# Ain't Your Money!

# Endorsements

In this book, Bob Bertelsen describes the natural process that facilitates the release of the supernatural power of God. Every believer must learn how to walk out these steps on his own with God so the supernatural provision will become a normal part of his life. I recommend this book to you because I know you will learn how to walk in his abundance for a lifetime as you follow what he teaches. He has also become a tremendous and loved conference teacher.

**Joan Hunter,** Joanhunter.org, Evangelist/Author, Host of Miracles Happen TV show

*******

Bob Bertelsen has been called by God to equip the Body of Christ to make money. This is important. Without finances, we cannot see the purposes of God done. Deuteronomy 8:18 tells us that the power to get wealth is for the intent of God's will being revealed in the earth. As you read this book, let the revelation of God empower you! I am convinced that the Lord is searching the earth to find those He can trust with this power. This book will help you be one of these!

**Robert Henderson,** Best-selling author of *The Courts of Heaven* series

*******

The foundational principles in *Ain't Your Money!* are not only related to wealth but can be applied to every area of life. The things Bob shares from the Bible and his own life experiences are proven keys to gaining success in every area. They are not just "good ideas" but Bible-based steps to move forward in your life and destiny. One of the things you will enjoy about this book is Bob's way of sharing in a practical and easy-to-read manner, just as spending time with a good friend. You will learn, be encouraged, and enjoy reading this book. It is one that can be shared with others, Bible-believing or not, and they will gain great life lessons. You will want to give it to others!

**Dr. John Benefiel,** Presiding Apostle - Heartland Apostolic Prayer Network**,** Founder and Senior Pastor - Church on the Rock, Oklahoma City

*******

Money is not what most people think it is. It's not something we acquire and hoard, or spend lavishly and cry for more when it's gone. Money, as Bob Bertelsen explains, is best understood as a force, either for good or evil. And that determination is up to us. Are we wise stewards? Or foolish stewards? Do we wish to hear "Well done, good and faithful servant"? Or, "You had one job! Just one!"

Find out the meaning of money as God intends it to be handled. Learn to be a good steward. Devour these pages and grow as your understanding of money grows. It's as important as learning to pray, praise, and love.

**Greg Hood**, Founder – Kingdom University, Franklin, Tennessee; Owner of TMS of Tennessee, LLC; Author of *The Gospel of the Kingdom, Sonship, Seed Wars, Ancient Evils–Present-Day Manifestations*

*******

In *Ain't Your Money!*, my friend Bob Bertelsen delivers a sharp, scriptural blueprint for anyone looking to move beyond the pressures of owning and into the freedom of stewarding. Having navigated the complexities of equity and real estate investing for many years, I find Bob's keys to stewardship to be an essential framework for ensuring that financial growth always serves a higher, kingdom purpose.

Bob's account of the 1988 fire is more than a business story—it's a masterclass in how a shifted perspective can turn a pile of ashes into a flourishing future. For those of us focused on building an inheritance for our children's children, this book provides the perfect mix of practical math—like the Rule of 72—and the spiritual maturity required to handle increase without losing your peace. This isn't just about making money; it's about honoring the True Provider at every level of the climb."

**Rhet Benefiel** Executive Pastor, Church on the Rock

*******

Bob is my husband, and I am delighted to endorse his third book. I can assure you that what he has said in this book not only has he lived it out, but he has also been taught directly by Holy Spirit how to implement each point. He is truly a man of Godly character.

**Laurie Bertelsen**, Wife, Life Coach, Founder of Attach For Life, author and speaker

*******

In his book, Bob shares how surrendering everything to God leads to real growth in our spiritual lives. He shows that true financial freedom comes when we steward God's resources well. This book is packed with practical, encouraging insights into the relationship between us, God, and money. If you want your finances to serve something far bigger than yourself, you're going to love this book.

**Tyler Ogden** – Estimator, A Plus Powder Coaters

Bob's mentorship and deep expertise have profoundly enriched my quality of life and significantly transformed my perception of wealth. His guidance has played a pivotal role in my personal, spiritual, and professional growth. If you're seeking to align your finances with a purpose beyond oneself, this book will resonate deeply with you and offer practical steps to unlock true prosperity through faithful stewardship of God.

**Steve Trimacco**, Quality Manager, A Plus Powder Coaters

*******

In his book, *Ain't Your Money!*, Bob has done an amazing presentation by revealing the truth of stewardship. His practical application from his life, sharing truth from the Bible, and presenting truths to apply in personal growth as a steward. Moving from financial slavery to a student, seeking a transformational mindset to a faithful steward who leads others in their journey to financial freedom.

**Dr. Charles Hamilton,** President of Harvest Preparation International Ministries, HPIM.

*******

This book puts words to something many of us have sensed but couldn't quite explain: that what we have isn't really ours; it's been entrusted to us. And once that clicks, it changes how you live. I love that it doesn't just talk about prosperity but brings it back to purpose and a Kingdom mindset. It gently challenges wrong thinking while pointing you back to a good and generous God, helping you walk in freedom with what He's placed in your hands.

**Andy Leong,** Heartland/Global Apostolic Prayer Network, Administrator

I've had the opportunity to work with Bob for nearly 15 years, and I can say with confidence that he truly lives out what he teaches. It's not just theory to him; it's how he operates. This book shows how he leads, how he makes decisions, and how he treats people. It's practical, grounded, and something you can actually apply, whether you're running a business or just trying to manage what you've been given a little better.

Some of what's in here can be tough to hear and even tougher to live out, but that's the point. The things that actually make a difference usually aren't the easy ones. If you're willing to put in the work and stay consistent, there's a lot in here that can genuinely change how you think and how you operate day to day.

**Nick Sukosd**, Operations Manager, A Plus Powder Coaters, Inc.

*******

Bob navigates the timeless complexities of modern faith, offering a refreshing, biblical perspective on stewardship through everyday struggles from humble beginnings to having to start a business all over from the ground up. This book is a timely wake-up call to live fully surrendered to Christ while being financially free. I highly recommend it for any believer looking to deepen their devotional life.

**Stephen M. Grant**, HR & Safety, A Plus Powder Coaters, Inc.

*******

I highly recommend this book to everyone who wants to know what God thinks about finances. We are called to be stewards of what is God's, not owners of what is ours. Bob Bertelsen gives us examples from scripture that point us to a theology of finances as well as several practical ways to apply these biblical principles. This isn't just theory. Bob lives what he believes every day and is an example of how to be a "good and faithful servant" by having faith, working hard, and increasing what God has entrusted to him.

**Ben Kibbe**, CEO, Kibbe Consulting

*******

I have had the privilege of knowing Bob personally for several years, and I can speak firsthand to the integrity, honesty, and unwavering faith that shape both his life and his work. In this book, Bob offers a thoughtful and deeply insightful perspective on stewardship, business, and finances while showing how these principles can be used to honor and serve our Lord and Savior. His wisdom on wealth and Jesus challenged and expanded my own understanding in powerful ways. Bob is a generous, grateful, and dedicated individual— truly faithful servant. "Well done, good and faithful servant."

**Dennis Reilly**, Friend

*******

Being an employee of A+ for the last 6 1/2 years, I've learned so much from Bob. He's not only my boss but has also become a trusted spiritual mentor and friend.

The principles of stewardship he shares in his book are straightforward, easy to understand, and apply to your life. More importantly, these principles are something Bob practices throughout his life on a daily basis. In reading this book, it has given me a new perspective on how to approach the things God has entrusted me with.

I considered it an honor and a privilege to be a part of A+ and its culture and to get to witness Bob's love for God and his commitment to helping others be their best!

**Heather Reilly**, Office Manager, A Plus Powder Coaters, Inc.

Bob Bertelsen's newest book, *Ain't Your Money!*, is easily digestible using clear thoughts, instructions, and insights into how prosperity should have a purpose aligned with God's kingdom. By adopting the right mindsets, actions, and characteristics, Bob Bertelsen outlines practical steps encouraging readers to grow in their abilities to steward the resources that God has provided for them. Bob shares his personal testimony of how God showed him faith-based principles to prosper financially, leaving a legacy for future generations.

**Melanie Sprouse**, Production Specialist Supervisor, A Plus Powder Coaters, Inc.

*******

Often, as humans, we are prone to resisting changing ourselves, often touting "that's just who I am!" That couldn't be further from the truth for Bob Bertelsen. I have watched him grow, change, and strive to be more God-like my entire life. And I have one of the best vantage points for that, because I am blessed to call him Dad.

**Angela McClaren**, daughter and former A Plus Powder Coaters, Inc employee

*******

Most Christians have a good basic understanding of eternal life and forgiveness. Unfortunately, many, if not most, Christians forget that this isn't the entire reason for Christ's sacrifice. John 10:10 says that he came so we could have life and life more abundantly. Bob does a great job of explaining stewardship, abundance and the blessings and responsibilities that come with it.

Reading this book and applying the thoughts and principles that are shared in it can be a key component to your growth as a believer and steward of God's resources. He includes actionable steps to bring you growth and success in your spiritual walk and financial journey.

I strongly recommend that you:

1. Buy this book
2. Buy a highlighter
3. Use them both and come back to them as your faith and responsibilities grow.

**Terry Watson**, Sales Manager, A Plus Powder Coaters, Inc., Christian Children's Author, Personal Finance Teacher

*******

Having known Bob his whole Christian life, I watched him grow from a self-absorbed, single guy who spent every dime on himself (or his trucks) to a caring, outrageous giver. Don't just read his stories and be inspired by His insights. Allow the Holy Spirit to change your own life, giving you prosperity with a purpose.

**Bruce Stryffeler**, friend, Pastor with Upper Room Fellowship

*******

*Ain't Your Money!* is a helpful continuation of Bob's previous books, *The Christian Entrepreneur* and *Created to Make Wealth.* Wrapping up the major components of effective stewardship in mindsets, actions, and characteristics, *Ain't Your Money!* looks to define healthy wealth. Bob isn't just interested in telling you; he's looking for active participation with his content through space given for prayer, repentance and contemplation. The cry continues into and through Bob's 3rd book: There is great purpose to our finances; our mindsets on wealth and stewardship matter hugely, and God wants to grow us not just in stewardship, but in character.

**Kate Holm**, Pastor, The Upper Room Fellowship

I've had the privilege of being the prayer intercessor for A Plus, Bob's company, since 2014. He offers nuggets of wisdom on how to handle our finances. He lives by the very principles he espouses in this book. All of us need to use our wealth to benefit others as well as ourselves.

Prosperity has a purpose for God's kingdom. After all, we are the trusted stewards of what He has given us.

**Linda Pera**, Intercessor for A Plus Powder Coaters, Inc.

*******

This book is an inspiring and theologically rich reminder that God owns everything and, as believers, we are stewards of what He has entrusted to us. Bob walks us through his journey and gives us a truly successful example of how to be good stewards for the Lord. His insight and testimony give us a wonderful blueprint for how to honor God through Biblical stewardship and open new levels of blessing. I highly recommend this book for anyone who wants to further honor God, grow God's Kingdom, and do their part financially with a spirit of excellence.

**Harold Zimmerman**, Alpha, Roofing and Construction, Inc. and an entrepreneur of 40 years

*******

I have known the author, Bob, for many years, and that personal connection has made reading his book on biblical stewardship especially meaningful and encouraging for me. Through his honest transparency and humble tone, Bob shares practical wisdom that feels like a loving conversation with a trusted friend. God disciplines those He loves Hebrews 12:6. His children today desperately need this kind of guidance. Bob's instructions are simple yet deeply thought-provoking. Am I actually doing these steps? Does my thinking about wealth truly align with God's Word?

I especially appreciated the emphasis on showing integrity, being trustworthy, and overflowing in generosity. These qualities are powerful evidence that God owns it all — and that we are called to steward well whatever He has entrusted to us. Reading this stirred a strong desire in me to one day hear the words of Jesus from Matthew 25:23: "His master replied, 'Well done, good and faithful servant! You have been faithful with a few things; I will put you in charge of many things. Come and share your master's happiness!'"

Bob is right — We must decide and act. This book has motivated me to examine my own heart and habits and to take concrete steps toward greater obedience and generosity.

**James Barton**, Pastor, Rush Church

*******

This *Key To Unlocking Peace, Purpose and Prosperity* is not just theory to Bob Bertelsen. In the nearly 20 years I have known Bob and Laurie, I have observed as they have been guided by these principles in both good times and bad. As they have faithfully walked the walk, these keys have unlocked finances for the kingdom projects around the world. I am confident that each one who reads and applies these keys will see the power of God to create wealth activated in their life for the purpose of advancing His Kingdom.

**Perry Chickonoski**, Pastor, Real Living Ministries

*******

Stewardship is more than a buzzword, it is more than a corporate slogan; stewardship is a core tenant of the Kingdom of God, it is the ethos that every spiritual pursuit of our lives. There is no one that I know who has a greater understanding of this Kingdom Principle than Bob Bertelsen. In his new book, "It Ain't Your Money", Bob walks us through a journey of wisdom and understanding on how to position ourselves to be entrusted with supernatural influence and resources to see the Kingdom of God advanced in the earth like never before. This is a how-to manual on wealth and stewardship for every believer.

**Dr. Kynan Bridges**, Best Selling Author, President of Kynan Bridges Ministries, Inc. Pastor of Grace & Peace Global Fellowship, Inc

*******

Everything Bob Bertelsen does ends up first class. He is an amazing individual. Everything I thought it took to be a success, to rise to the top, has been upended by his example. He is the true testament to what God does in the heart of a soul that bends a knee to him.

They say the true test of a relationship is not when things are going right, but when things go wrong. I remember vividly the day I was sitting with my wife at an outdoor café in Colorado Springs, enjoying the mountain spring day.

My phone lit up. Bob was calling me.

"Hey Jim! How do you spell *Entrepreneur*?"

My gut turned to stone. It had been three weeks since publishing his latest book, *The Christian Entrepreneur*. The cover was wrong.

I said a few *Hail Marys* (OK, so maybe that's not how I spelled 'hail') and begged forgiveness as I outlined a plan for correction. Bob was so gracious, even to the point of finding the humor in the situation. (He more than I.)

It's times like those that make you want to give your best to someone. Not a person demanding perfection, but rather, a person demonstrating perfection.

I still can't spell *Entrepreneur*, (I had to look it up for this endorsement), but I know how to spell friend: B-O-B.

Thank you, Bob. And may God bless you and all that you do.

**Jim Bryson**, Editor, Publisher, Writing Coach; Author of *Who Shot Your Tail Off? A Writer's Guide to Passion, Purpose, Production and Staying Alive.*

*******

Bob Bertlesen is the type of person who makes possible the things that I do. While I'm preaching in a the jungle somewhere, or riding in a desert vehicle surrounded by Pakistan soldiers, or preaching under the cover of armed security guards with fire in their eyes, Bob is back home doing what he does best—building wealth, and building people.

I can't say I've ever seen Bob in the middle of a desert, but if I did, he'd probably be driving a souped-up Humvee and racing camels.

Bob, thank you for all that you do. You are truly the shaft that drives the spear.

**Dr. Harold Eberle**, Prophet, Theologian, Author of several books, including *Father-Son Theology, Who is God?* and *Precious in His Sight.*

# Ain't Your Money!

*******************

## *Stewardship, The Key to Unlocking Peace, Purpose and Prosperity*

*Bob Bertelsen*

# Copyright

## Ain't Your Money!

by Bob Bertelsen



Editing and Layout by Jim Bryson and Nora Bryson

Graphics by David Munoz (davidmunoznvtn@gmail.com)

# Contents

# Dedication

I FIRST DEDICATE THIS BOOK to my Lord and Savior. I believe if it were not for God's grace and mercy, I would have never survived to be sixty-five. He has seen me through fires that burned my business to the ground, the flooding of a new office, and many more obstacles. No matter the adversity, he has been faithful to teach me and see me through the hardships. The good season far outweighs the adversity that we have gone through. Thank you, Lord, for the path you have taken me down. Thank you for the opportunity to share the things you have taught me in life. I pray it helps others change their perspective on money.

# Acknowledgements

WHAT A GOOD THING when a man finds a Godly woman. I am so blessed to have found such a woman. Laurie, you are so amazing! There is no one else I would have rather been on this journey than with you. You have stood by me in good and bad times. You have encouraged me in all my business endeavors and walked through them with me. I am so honored you said yes to marrying me. I wouldn't want to do life with anyone else. Thank you for your support, prayers and love. I love you!

I want to thank the staff at A Plus Powder Coaters, Inc. Wow, am I blessed with an amazing management team and I get to work with them. They handle all the day-to-day things, so I can spend time writing, speaking, racing and building cars, and working on the business. I know they have everything under control. They do an amazing job.

Terry Watson (A+ sales manager) has been with me for about 28 years. You have had my back and given everything you have to make sure A+ succeeds. You treat A+ like it is your own and make decisions that are what is best for A+. I know A+ would not be at the place it is without you.

Nick Sukosd (A+ operations manager). I remember when I first met you, I saw your work ethic and the hustle you had, and I told Laurie, "I want him to work at A+." It has been 14 years, and boy, did I get it right in picking you to come to work for A+. Actually, I think God picked you and had you in mind to work here. Thanks for your endless pursuit of making the shop run at its best. You do an awesome job.

Steve (A+ Quality Manager) and Tyler (A+ Estimating). You both worked so hard as laborers and gave it your all. You are proof that working hard will lead to advancement. Steve, you came right out of high school, a little shy, but willing to give it your all. Now you are my quality manager. Tyler, you came and worked hard, too. You left and came back. When you returned, I saw in you the qualities we needed in management and put you in estimating. You guys represent our values well.

Heather (A+ office manager) and Mel (A+ production Specialist supervisor). Heather, thank you for keeping our accounting straight, taking care of the office and keeping me on task and not late for appointments. Mel, thank you for all you do, from answering the phones, entering work orders, straightening out paperwork, and keeping production entries correct. You do a great job! You two do an amazing job running the office.

All the A+ employees. You guys are the best! You work not only hard at production, but you work to keep our values. I brag about my amazing co-workers everywhere I go. I think I am the most blessed man to work with such awesome people. You are A+'s greatest asset. Thank you for all you do!!!!

I want to thank Pastors Joy & Perry Chickonoski for their spiritual covering and encouragement to share what God has done at A+. Also, Pastor Chuck Hamilton for his encouragement and support when I attended his church.

Robert Henderson, you have been a divine appointment in my life. You have helped promote me and get me in front of people at many of your events. I am so thankful for our alignment and your friendship.

Joan Hunter, we met at a conference I was speaking at, and you only had a minute and came, handed me your card and said call me next week, I need you to speak at my conference in March. Little did

I know you would become a great friend. You were a divine appointment as well.

Harold Eberle, your help in introducing me to Jim Bryson, who edited the first, second, and now the third book. You encouraged me to tell my story and help transform lives. Thank you.

Jim Bryson, Harold gave me your phone number, and the first time I called, I knew we would work well together. Our introduction in writing has led to someone I thoroughly enjoy talking to. We have great conversations about politics, business, racing, bikes, and cars. When it comes to editing and writing, you make me sound really good. I know my books are much better because you had your hand in them. Thank you.

Mark & Sheri, you are some of Laurie's and my closest friends. We eat out, play cards, travel, just to mention a few things. We enjoy our time together. I appreciate Mark's perspective on business, as he is in business. Thanks for all the help and encouragement over the years.

God, you are so amazing! Only you would take a small, shy boy with no formal education who barely passed high school, create a businessman, then have me write my story and speak in front of people. You have great plans for us. Thank you for the path you have taken me down!

# Foreword

## *By Lance Wallnau*

I DON'T USUALLY WRITE FOREWORDS. When I wrote my first book, my editor told me, "Don't worry, most people skip the Foreword."

If you're still reading, you're already in a different category.

That matters, because this book isn't written for the crowd. It's written for the few God can trust with influence, responsibility…and money.

Let's be honest: Most Christians have a conflicted, confused relationship with money. They quote Scripture about it, worry about it, need it, but rarely understand it. And almost never master it.

Bob Bertelsen does.

Early in this manuscript, he says something that will either offend you or set you free:

"I love working in the marketplace. I love managing people. And I love making money. (Please notice: I love making money; I don't love money.)"

Most believers won't say that out loud. Bob does because he understands the difference.

He doesn't love money. He loves what money does when it's in the hands of someone aligned with God.

Here's what I've observed about people like Bob: they don't see money the way most people do. To them, it's not primarily about comfort, consumption, or security. It's a scoreboard. A feedback system. A measurable way to track whether they are multiplying what God put in their hands.

They've effectively "gamified" stewardship.

While others stress over bills, they're studying numbers—sales, margins, growth—not as a burden, but as a challenge. A test. A calling. And here's the part that really separates them: they have just as much fun giving money as they do making it.

That's a different mindset entirely.

So, what is Bob's real business?

He answers it without hesitation:

"I was created to make wealth so I can partner with ministries and finance what they are called to do."

A Kingdom financier.

That language may sound unusual, but it's biblical, necessary, and overdue.

God has a plan for your prosperity. Most people don't see God's plan, but Bob's life follows these stages.

- Sufficiency – no longer dependent on others (1 Thess 4:12)
- Prosperity – meet your needs and give (1 Cor 16:2)
- Wealth – the capacity to do even more (Mt 27:57-60)
- The Ministry of Finance – becoming a pipeline God can trust (1 Chron 29:2)

Most people stop at survival. Some reach stability. A remnant step into generosity.

But few step into the role of Kingdom Financier.

Bob has.

And more importantly, he shows you how to do the same.

He doesn't hide the mistakes. He doesn't sanitize the process. He walks you through the real journey—what works, what breaks, and what it actually takes to move from one level to the next.

So, here's the question:

Are you content to think about money the way everyone else does?

Or are you ready to see it the way God does, and step into the responsibility that comes with it?

If it's the second, don't skim this book.

Study it.

**Lance Wallnau**, Speaker, Author, CEO Lance Learning Group

# 1

# Early Days

I'M FIVE YEARS OLD, sitting in my chair, eating Animal Crackers, and listening to the Sunday School teacher tell the story of some rich man who was going on a journey. Before he left, however, he entrusted part of his money to his three servants. When he came back, he wanted to know how each servant handled his portion of the money. The story concluded with the praise: "Well done, good and faithful servant."

That is my first memory of Matthew 25, *The Parable Of The Bags Of Gold.*

Fast forward about ten years, and I get saved during the tail end of the "Jesus People Movement." I'm on fire for God, wanting more of him. I go from a pessimist who hates life, thinking no one loves me, not even my parents, no purpose to loving life, to an optimist who finds his purpose, knowing God loves me. It's a huge shift in my life. I start reading the Bible, praying daily, and trying to learn all I can about God and his plan for my life.

Now I'm 19 when I hear a pastor talk on Matthew 25, *The Parable Of The Bags Of Gold.* Only this time, no Animal Crackers. Part of it is the "Well done, good and faithful servant" ending. For some reason, this really gets my attention. Probably because I don't think of myself as good or faithful. I feel like a sinner who loves Jesus and keeps on screwing up.

One day, I opened to Matthew 25 and read "Well done, good and faithful servant." I can't get the thought out of my mind. I picture myself on Judgement Day, standing before Father God, head down, fingers crossed, and hoping to hear those words: "Well done, good and faithful servant. Enter into the joy of your Lord."

I imagine we all long to hear these words at the end of our lives, signifying that we have done well, been found faithful, and are welcomed into heaven.

> *His master replied, "Well done, good and faithful servant! You have been faithful with a few things; I will put you in charge of many things. Come and share your master's happiness!"*
>
> Matthew 25:21

This is the first scripture I associate with stewardship. Nearly everyone who speaks or writes about stewardship uses this scripture. I, too, will be using it throughout this book. My thoughts on stewardship have evolved through the years that I have been studying and teaching the subject. God keeps downloading more revelation about it. Originally, I taught on the three *principles* that I felt encompassed stewardship. A couple of years ago, God showed me three *actions* that stewards take. And lately, God showed me three *characteristics* of a good steward.

So I felt it was time to write a new book on stewardship and the nine keys God has shown me over the years. I do not claim to know everything about stewardship, but I want to share what I do know.

**Leaving Something Behind**

> *A good person leaves an inheritance for their children's children.*
>
> Proverbs 13:22

Part of this inheritance is wealth. Yet it is hard to leave wealth for your grandchildren when you are poor. It takes quite a bit of wealth to have enough for your own lifetime, your children's lifetime, and still have enough for your grandchildren. The reality is that the average person does not leave enough for their children, let alone their grandchildren. The good news, however, is that stewardship brings increase to our finances. Through being a good steward, we are blessed with more to steward, and that enables giving.

I don't want to step on any toes this early in the book (maybe later in the book), but many people don't have the financial resources to leave their grandchildren wealth because they don't steward what they have. They spend their whole lives living paycheck to paycheck, only having enough for today.

Before diving into stewardship and how it is the foundation for wealth increase, however, let me tell you of my struggles with money in the early years.

**My Story**

I got saved at age 14. I worked at Ace Hardware from age 14 to 16, fixing broken windows and screens, stocking shelves and doing occasional sales. At 16, I started working in a factory during the summers, which led to full-time employment once I graduated high school. (More accurately, I left high school and they were generous enough to give me a diploma.)

When I got married at 23, I was still working at the factory. My wife, Laurie, and I struggled financially in our first few years. Our combined income in 1984 was $14,000 and change. That is not a lot of money, then or now. In 1986, I was promoted to management with a fifty percent increase in my wages. The next year, my wages doubled, then doubled the year after that. Then I was offered a chance to buy a third of the company. I was making six figures before I was thirty.

That six-figure income came with some struggles. I heard in church that you shouldn't be wealthy, that poverty was next to Godliness. This led to an existential crisis.

*Am I a sinner because I made six figures?*
*Is my salvation in jeopardy because of this wealth?*
*Am I going to hell because they paid me so much?*
*What should I do? Tell them not to pay me so much?*

None of this made sense, so I started praying. I asked God to show me what to do with the wealth I was earning, and if it was even ok to have wealth in the first place. The first scripture I read about wealth was in Matthew.

> *As evening approached, there came a rich man from Arimathea, named Joseph, who had himself become a disciple of Jesus.*
>
> Matthew 27: 57

Here was a rich man who was a disciple of Jesus. Why would Jesus let a rich man be his disciple if wealth was wrong? This scripture was very freeing to me. I began to see that wealth isn't bad.

> *But remember the Lord your God, for it is he who gives you the ability to produce wealth, and so confirms his covenant, which he swore to your ancestors, as it is today.*
>
> Deuteronomy 8:18

This scripture says God gives us the ability to produce wealth. Why would he give us that ability if we were not intended to produce wealth? That would be a cruel joke—you can make wealth, but you can't keep it. God isn't like that. When he says he gives us the ability to produce wealth, we can assume that he also gives us the ability to steward that wealth without getting a big head and thinking we are more than we are.

I discovered another scripture that shows it is ok to have wealth. This recounts how King David allocated a portion of his vast wealth.

> *Besides, in my devotion to the temple of my God I (David) now give my personal treasures of gold and silver for the temple of my God, over and above everything I have provided for this holy temple: three thousand talents of gold (gold of Ophir) and seven thousand talents of refined silver, for the overlaying of the walls of the buildings, for the gold work and the silver work.*
>
> 1 Chronicles 29: 3-5

By today's standards, David's gift is valued at twenty billion dollars. Yes, *billion.* Notice what God says about David.

> *After removing Saul, he made David their king. God testified concerning him: 'I have found David son of Jesse, a man after my own heart; he will do everything I want him to do.'*
>
> Acts 13:22

Here is David, a man after God's own heart, giving away twenty billion dollars. It stands to reason, then, that if David gave away such a sum, he had it in the first place. (Clearly, David did not operate like the United States government.)

With these scriptures tucked away in my heart, I felt relieved. It was ok to acquire wealth as long as I stewarded carefully.

**Financer of the Kingdom**

Recently, I was a speaker for the *Unleashing Heaven Wealth Conference* at Joan Hunter Ministries in Tomball, Texas. As the title implies, it was a conference about prosperity and increase. Robert Henderson, Barber Wentroble, Kynan Bridges and Mark Kauffman were also speakers. Robert, Mark and I began chatting in the green room before the conference. Mark made a comment that struck me.

He said that all the prosperity teachers of the past—Oral Roberts, Kenneth Copeland, Benny Hinn, to mention a few—had great prosperity messages but lacked a purpose.

That resonated with me.

I realized that in the late 1980s, I struggled with justifying making money until God showed me the scriptures in Matthew 27:57 and Deuteronomy 8:18. Yet I was also struggling with my calling. You see, in the church of young believers who got saved during the Jesus movement, there was a theme of: What is your calling?

At the time, I thought a calling was to be a pastor, evangelist or missionary. I didn't really want to be any of those; I had no desire at all. But because of the pressure of the church, I started to pray about it. I still did not want to be any of those callings, but yielding to God, I said, "I surrender. If you want me to be a pastor, evangelist or missionary, I'll do it…but I won't like it."

I felt God say, "NO!"

My response was, "Thank you, Jesus!"

So if my calling wasn't to be a pastor, evangelist or missionary, what was it?

Well…I love working in the marketplace. I love managing people. And I love making money. (Please notice: I love *making money*; I don't love money.) But I still wondered: *What is my calling?*

Finally, God answered. He said I was a "Financer of the Kingdom."

*A what?*

Let me explain. Every ministry, whether it is a community church, missionary network, evangelistic outreach, or anything, requires finances to fulfill its destiny. I was created to make wealth so I can partner with ministries and finance what they are called to do. In other words, giving to their ministry fulfills my calling, and it allows them to fulfill their calling. We both accomplish what we were called to do. They do what they love. I do what I love. It is a beautiful partnership.

When Mark made the comment that the prosperity gospel was missing a purpose, I realized I had the purpose. I had been doing it, living it and embracing it for about forty years—financing the kingdom. As I like to say, "Earthly Wealth for Kingdom Purpose." That is the major purpose of producing wealth.

**Bread and Seed**

Now, lest you think all wealth has to be given away, that isn't what I'm saying. We are to keep some and give some. It is up to each of us to ask God how much we are to give away and how much we are to keep.

I have heard several pastors explain it like this:

> From wheat, we get grain, which we can plant as seed or grind into flour for bread. So the flour, we will call bread, which is something we eat.
>
> We cannot take all of the grain, grind it into flour and eat all the bread. If we did, we would have nothing for the next season. If we planted all the grain, we would have nothing to eat now and would starve to death.

There is a balance between bread and seed. It is the same with finances. If we give it all away, we have nothing for our bills now. Yet if we don't sow (give some of the finances away), we will have nothing for the future. It is up to each of us to ask God what part of our wealth is seed and what part is bread.

I know what this proportion is for Laurie and me. I never spend my seed—the money I am to sow into kingdom purpose. Likewise, I don't give away what God has blessed me with. Still, at times, God has called me to sow my bread as a test of obedience. He once asked me if I loved him more than the bank account I had established. After talking with Laurie, we felt he was asking us to give it away. Which we did.

Of course, there are good-hearted people who struggle with keeping even a portion of what God gives them. *How can I have nice things when the world is starving? I could feed the poor with the money I was going to use to buy a car.*

This mindset stems from thinking God is low on resources; that God is running out of money. In fact, God is an endless source. We read from God's Word:

> *The earth is the Lord's, and everything in it, the world, and all who live in it.*
>
> Psalm 24:1

Thinking that God doesn't have enough comes from a poverty mindset.

- God can't provide.
- He is going broke.
- We are not worthy to have nice things.
- We don't deserve them.

I agree in part: We don't deserve God's blessings. Our sinful nature makes us unworthy. Yet God loves us and sent his son, Jesus, to die for our sins. That makes us children of God. I am, and you are, a child of God. As a dad in my family, I love to give my children not only the things they need, but also some of the things they want. God is the same with us.

**Poverty Mindset**

A few years back, I bought a Camaro 2SS RS Convertible for Laurie and I to go on date nights. It was not my primary vehicle; it was an extra car…for enjoyment.

At church one Sunday, someone asked me, "When did you get that?"

My response was reflexive.

"I got a really great deal on it," I blurted out. "I bought it in my dealership, so I didn't pay sales tax, and I plan to flip it (sell it for more than I paid) in the fall."

Upon further reflection, I realized that I didn't answer their question. Instead, I tried to justify my purchase. *It was a great deal! An investment! Have you seen the engine?*

In fact, I was operating out of a poverty mindset by putting a ceiling on what was an acceptable level for God to bless me. A few years later, God told me I needed to repent for my poverty mindset.

Think about it as a parent. You know your children really want something. It's a little expensive, so you save and cut back until you can afford it. You give it to them, then you hear them tell their friends, "Mom and Dad got a really good deal on it. They had a coupon. It was double coupon day. And when I'm done with it, I'm gonna sell it and they will get their money back."

Wouldn't that hurt? You worked hard. You wanted to bless them. And they are making excuses to justify your gift.

I think God is a little offended when we justify our purchases. He wants to bless us, and instead, we devalue it.

I shared my story of that Camaro at a conference. This led to a time of repentance for our poverty mindsets. During that time, God showed me that a poverty mindset is a ceiling on what God can give and do in our lives. It limits us from enjoying what God wants to bless us with.

From this repentance, my old ceiling got raised. I was above worrying about what people think about my extra cars, our nice home, flying first class, etc. I actually thought I had no ceiling left and the sky was the limit…until:

*What if God blessed me with a private jet? Would I feel compelled to justify it? I could say that Laurie and I travel a lot, and there are always multiple airports for us. It could save us 5-8 hours of travel time.*

Yet that would be justifying it.

I felt convicted. I had raised my ceiling, but I still had a ceiling.

I repented again and asked forgiveness.

Someday I may have a private plane, maybe even a jet, and if God wants to bless me with it, I will use it for his purposes. I would love to travel that way and be able to bless others with it as well, especially my editor! (*Nice one, Jim.*) I believe God is able to do it if that is his will for me, but it won't happen until my ceiling has been obliterated.

So, to be perfectly clear, I believe in the prosperity message, but I believe it must have a purpose—a kingdom purpose. If there is no purpose, we become the purpose. When we become the purpose, we start loving money.

> *For the love of money is a root of all kinds of evil. Some people, eager for money, have wandered from the faith and pierced themselves with many griefs.*
>
> 1 Timothy 6:10

When we love money, it causes us to wander from our faith. That becomes the root of all kinds of evil.

> *No one can serve two masters; for either he will hate the one and love the other, or else he will be loyal to the one and despise the other. You cannot serve God and mammon.*
>
> Matthew 6:24 NKJV

Mammon: "wealth regarded as an evil influence or false object of worship and devotion." (Dictionary Oxford Languages)

When wealth is just for us—our selfish purposes—it becomes *mammon*: a false object of worship. We are called to worship God. No one or anything else. Our focus is God, period.

**Nine Keys**

This book will give you a good scriptural understanding of stewardship. It will give you nine keys to stewardship, which will position you for financial increase. And it will give you a good foundation to keep finances in perspective. God's perspective.

Throughout this book, I will talk about two companies I have stewarded: Therm-O-Cel Company, which is the first company I bought and then sold in 2009. And A Plus Powder Coaters, Inc., which Laurie and I founded in 1996, and as of this writing, we still steward.

This book will address stewarding our finances and seeing an increase in our finances. Every one of us, if we are honest with ourselves, would like to see more money in our lives.

- Having more money for things we want.
- Be able to live debt-free.
- Be able to bless others financially.

The three principles, three actions and three characteristics I am going to lay out will be the foundation we all need to steward more finances and see an increase in our finances.

I pray God speaks to you through this book and brings financial increase to you and your family.

# Part I

# Mindsets

*Owner, Provider, Steward*

# 2

# Owner

## *It's God's, Not Mine*

IF YOU HAVE HEARD ME SPEAK or read my other books, then you are aware of my three mindsets of a steward. I have been speaking and writing on this for many years. Even if you are familiar with these, however, I encourage you not to skip these early chapters, as they may refresh your memory or even teach you something new.

> Stewardship: "The conducting, supervising, or *managing* of something; especially the careful and responsible management of something *entrusted* to one's care."

Consider two key words in this definition.

*Managing* means "to take care of something."

*Entrusted* implies that someone else owns whatever we have been entrusted with.

If I am entrusted with the maintenance of a home, for example, it means I don't own it. Rather, I am entrusted to take care of it for the owner.

When it comes to wealth, who owns it? Is it ours? Do we own it? Strange as it may sound, we don't own anything. Psalm 24:1 tells us as much:

> *The earth is the Lord's, and everything in it, the world, and all who live in it.*

Does that include our wealth? Scripture says:

> *"The silver is mine and the gold is mine," declares the Lord Almighty.*
>
> Haggai 2:8

Clearly, the silver and gold are God's. And silver and gold represent money. At one point in the United States of America, our currency was backed by gold. So, God is telling us our money is his.

David goes a step further.

> *Yours, O Lord, is the greatness and the power and the glory and majesty and the splendor, for everything in heaven and earth is yours.*
>
> 1 Chronicles 29:11

Are you seeing a pattern? God owns everything. He not only created heaven and earth, but he also owns heaven and earth. Earth includes our homes, cars, money, all our cool stuff, and anything else we have. We own absolutely nothing.

When I first realized I owned nothing, I came up with this reminder:

| IT'S GOD'S<br>NOT MINE |
|---|

I wrote it on a Post-It note and put it on my mirror to read every morning. I needed to change my mindset from "I own stuff" to believing and thinking "God owns everything."

I have since made wristbands that say, "IT'S GOD'S, NOT MINE." I wear it to help me remember that God owns everything.

When my oldest daughter was eight years old, I told her:

> "Sweetheart, at some point, you are going to get mad at us and want to run away from home. I need you to understand that you came to us with nothing, and you will leave with nothing.
>
> When you run away, leave your clothes at the back door, as they are not yours; Mom and I bought them. As a loving, caring father, I suggest that if you choose to run away, you do it in the summer, as our winters are brutal, and I don't want you to get frostbite."

Now, I was just teasing my daughter, but isn't that how we are with God? We came here with nothing, and we will leave here with nothing. It is all his. Nothing is ours.

Do you have the perspective of God who owns everything? Or are you stuck claiming everything as your own?

Here's another perspective.

Claiming we own something that really isn't ours is considered stealing. If I were caught driving your car without permission, you could say I stole your car, and I would be arrested. It is the same with taking possession of the things God owns.

Let's take a minute for repentance. Pray this prayer before moving on to the next chapter.

**Prayer**

Father, I declare that you own everything, "for everything in heaven and earth is yours" (1 Chronicles 29:11).

This tells me everything—including my home, my car and all assets I thought I owned—are really yours. Forgive me for taking ownership of your possessions. Help me have the correct mindset that: "It is Yours, not mine." Amen!

# 3

# Provider

## *My Future Up In Smoke*

WE HAVE ESTABLISHED that we are not the owner. Who is the provider?

For several generations, men have been considered the providers of the home. We are supposed to work hard, bring home the bacon, and hand it to the wife. But is that really scriptural? Did God create Adam to work in the garden all day and bring home produce for Eve?

Let's explore what the Bible says about the provider.

> *Consider the ravens: They do not sow or reap, they have no storeroom or barn; yet God feeds them. And how much more valuable you are than birds! Who of you by worrying can add a single hour to your life?*
>
> Luke 12:24-25

First, let us look at a comparison that is made in this scripture. God says we are more valuable than birds. But wait! Did God send his only son to die for the sins of black birds or ravens? Not exactly. When you think of the hierarchy of birds, ravens are not very high up on the list. (Although folks in Baltimore would take issue with that.) Most people looking for a pet bird seek cockatiels, parrots or other exotic birds, not black birds or ravens. In fact, in Ohio, where I live, when the crows/ravens take off from a cornfield, the sky can get dark.

There are thousands of them. The raven is a monetarily worthless bird.

The comparison is to us—the believers, the ones that God actually sent his only son to die for. When Jesus died for our sins, we were adopted as children of God. This means we are royalty, sons and daughters of the King of Kings, princes and princesses of the Lord God Almighty. That is a stark contrast to ravens. But consider the underlying meaning: if God values a near-worthless bird enough to provide for it, surely, he will take abundant care of his beloved children.

In verse twenty-five, he says, "Who of you by worrying can add a single hour to your life?" The answer is: No one. In fact, doctors are now saying that ninety percent of sickness and disease is caused by stress and worry. The good news is this: If you adapt my stewardship message, you will be healthier and live longer! I guarantee it!

**Provider**

From Genesis 22:14

> *So Abraham called that place THE LORD WILL PROVIDE. And to this day it is said, "On the mountain of the Lord it will be provided."*

This scripture uses the Hebrew word *Jehovah-Jireh* for God. It means: "The Lord will provide." Providing is part of God's nature; it's in his very name. Indeed, we are told he will provide for all our needs.

> *And my God will meet all your needs according to the riches of his glory in Christ Jesus.*
>
> Philippians 4:19

Interestingly, Americans have a hard time separating needs and wants. Our basic needs include a roof over our heads, clothing, food and water. Our wants go a bit further: two cars, a TV in every room, heated toilet seats, and a fine trim lawn. To be candid, I am so glad I serve a God who not only wants to meet my needs but also supplies some of my wants. It's a matter of maturity.

As we steward well, God entrusts us with more things, especially when we have the right perspective: "It's God's, not mine."

Yes, God supplies all our needs and can also supply our wants. For instance, in addition to my everyday cars, God has blessed me with two classic Corvettes, two classic Camaros, and a 1978 GMC Jimmy. I know he has provided them, and he is the owner. I am just lucky enough to get to drive them. (Turns out, God is a car guy too. How cool is that?)

**Humble Beginnings**

When I was 16, I started working for the Therm-O-Cel company, a small factory. When I graduated from high school, my dad really wanted me to go to college. He often said, "You can lose all your money, but you can never lose your education." There is truth to that, but for me, school was difficult. I struggle to read and comprehend things. I barely graduated from high school, so I continued to work as a laborer in this factory.

I met Laurie when I was twenty, and we married three years later in 1984. We had a combined income of $14,000 our first year together and were quite poor for a few years afterwards. We bought a used mobile home, drove a used Chevette and a beat-up Oldsmobile Delta 88. We cut grass and firewood to make ends meet.

Date night, when we could afford it, was a two-dollar meal from Chi Chi's Cantina. We'd sit at the bar where they had free chips, salsa and refried beans. We each got a pop for seventy-five cents, and we left a fifty-cent tip. Date night on a budget!

In 1986, the owner of the Therm-O-Cel company decided to sell his business. He had an interested buyer coming to the shop for a tour.

Before I go on, let me describe the business. We made exothermic compounds for the steel industry. These are dry powders that, when ignited, will burn at about 3,000 degrees. We mixed and bagged the powders for the steel mills. It was an extremely dirty, dusty environment. I wore coveralls, a hat and a respirator. I'd come home from work filthy and immediately take a shower. The water by my feet would turn black.

The day that the potential buyers came to see the facility, I was working in the mixing and packaging area. As usual, I was covered in dust. I came up to the workshop for my five-minute break, and the owner introduced me to the two men taking the tour. Just as he did, the owner got paged to a phone call and left me to talk with these men. We had a conversation on how things worked and how I was trained by the foreman to repair equipment. (I may not be good at bookwork, but I can tear apart and rebuild just about anything.) When the owner returned, I went back to work, thinking nothing more of the conversation.

Now would probably be a good time to mention that the owner of the Therm-O-Cel company was my dad. Of course, you are probably thinking I was a shoo-in to own the company, but that would be far from the truth. My dad would never give a company to me. He might sell it. But he didn't think I was smart enough to run the company anyway, because I had not gone to college.

It just so happened that Laurie and I were invited to my parents' house for dinner, an occasion that meant real meat for a change. (We didn't get much meat on our meager budget, and I am a carnivore.)

We sat down for dinner and Dad said:

"What did you tell those potential buyers today?"

*Uh oh. I'm in trouble.*

Dad continued: "They told me, if they bought the business, it would be contingent on you staying and running it."

This, apparently, was an eye-opener for Dad. As I said, he thought I needed college to amount to anything. Now, strangers were telling him I was capable of running his company.

The potential buyers never bought the company, but my dad now offered me a chance to buy it. Yes, *buy* it; not *give* it to me. As we discussed it, I told Dad I wanted to start a family, and I did not want to be absent from my children's lives the way he had been absent from our lives. Dad worked around the clock. Out of town on sales calls during the day, then paying bills, scheduling production, and designing new equipment in the evening. I know my dad loved me, but he never attended any of my junior high sporting events or spent personal time with me.

I didn't want that for my family. I wanted to spend more time with my children.

After some thought and prayer, I realized I was interested in running production and purchasing, and I'd let someone else handle sales. It just so happened that a few days later, Bill Dawson—someone my dad had tried to hire twenty-plus years ago for sales—called the office. He was just reaching out to my dad to see if we might need someone in sales. We hired Bill for a probationary period of one year to see if Bill and I could get along. The plan was that if we could work together, the three of us: Dad, Bill, and I, would each buy a third of the company.

Bill was a rock star salesman. Dad had let the company dwindle because he wanted to retire. Bill came with energy and set the sales on fire. Because I had spent so many years in the shop, I started making changes to the way we manufactured products. I increased daily productivity by three times. Soon, the business was more productive and profitable than ever. Running on all eight cylinders, so to speak.

In mid-1987, we had a handshake deal for Dad, Bill and I to each own a third of the company. In January, we still had no formal deal, but the attorneys were working on it. Meanwhile, Laurie was pregnant with our first child. The company was doing better than ever in sales and production.

Then everything changed.

**Flames of Revival**

It was the end of May, a cool, partly cloudy morning. Bill was forty-five minutes away, waiting for me to deliver a pallet of our company's product for a sample run at a new customer's facility. Dad was in Pittsburgh visiting another customer. He was re-energized when Bill started selling so much, so he went to an old customer to see if he could drum up some new business.

I had just finished setting a pallet of product on my pickup truck when an employee came running up the ramp to the dock yelling, "Fire, Fire! Fire in the production area."

I wasn't too concerned, because these employees could exaggerate a bit. As I walked quickly through the building to the production area, I detected smoke, and then I saw four fire extinguishers on the ground. The employees had emptied them trying to extinguish the fire. Turning the corner, I saw it, a real fire: 15 feet wide, 25 feet long, and 20 feet high. The flames were touching the roof.

I knew we were in trouble. Built in the late 1800s, the building consisted of cinder-block walls, wooden beams, and decking. Old wood loves to burn.

Now, fire requires three components. The first is an ignition source. I didn't know what set this fire off, but it was past the ignition stage. The second component is fuel. This fire not only had wood to burn, but it also had aluminum powder, which is a particularly hot-burning fuel. The third component is oxygen. There is oxygen in the air, but if you want a really hot burning fire, you add extra oxygen. We had sodium nitrate, which is an oxidizer—it adds oxygen to fire. We made exothermic compounds that burn at 3,000 degrees F, and this was the area where many of the chemicals were mixed.

All this to say: That fire was burning hot and fast.

Fortunately for us, the Leetonia volunteer fire department was right next door. The call went out, and after what seemed like hours, Clarence, the fire chief and one other guy arrived in the fire department's pickup truck. Clarence was pushing 70—some said pushing it hard. He probably tested 80 a few times and rejected it. When he and his partner pulled up, the flames were through the roof, blazing about 25 feet over the building. I ran up to the truck, and Clarence said, "Bob, this fire is too big for us."

*You think?* Two firefighters in a pickup, and we have a hundred-year-old building blazing.

Before long, we had five fire departments and over 80 firemen on the scene. Three local TV stations sent film crews out. (In 1988, there were no smartphones with a camera to video the fire.) The fire chiefs and fire marshals were all asking questions. At one point, they asked me to drive a forklift into an area where the fire had been extinguished, but I thought there may be embers still burning behind some product. I moved pallets out of the way. I was busy with questions from the firemen and news reporters. Laurie showed up and now I had one more thing to worry about: my pregnant wife and our unborn child.

The firemen got the fire extinguished around 3 pm. They had brought in portable water storage tanks and were now taking them down. Others were rolling up fire hoses. As things calmed down for me, I walked over to our storage building, which, miraculously, was still standing.

The building was elevated so trucks could dump their semi loads of material into the bins below. This put me eye-level with the roofline of the burned building, except there was no roof. Our whole production area had burned up. Fortunately, our raw material building and finished-goods building were unscathed. Yet our production area was gone, including over thirty motors—the ones we used to mix the product.

As I gazed where the roof had been, a puff of smoke and embers rolled out of the building. Reality hit me hard. My whole future had just gone up in smoke. This business was my path out of poverty, and now it was gone. With a child on the way, I had been working for the last year and a half to build something that would provide for my family. Now that bright future was a pile of ashes.

I was upset. No…let's be real, I was MAD! The firemen were rolling up their hoses twenty feet away, and I didn't want them to hear me, so I gritted my teeth and muttered, "God! How could you do this to me?" Oh, was I incensed. And in that moment, he broke me. I heard God speak in an audible voice so loud, I thought everyone for miles around heard it too. I couldn't believe the firemen didn't stop and look to the sky.

God said, "I give the blessing, and I can take it away!"

I knew at that moment, at 27 years of age, I was a monument unto myself. I thought I was hot stuff, being a business owner, increasing production, seeing my wages go from $14,000 a year to six figures. I was full of myself, but in that moment, I was broken. I thought I was the provider. I thought it was by my own abilities that the company was prospering. The revelation of that moment was that it is God who prospers us. It is God who has the ability to bless or withhold blessing.

I was staggered. I quickly repented for my arrogance and pride.

I have told this story many times, and it never fails to affect me. It is an Ebenezer moment for me. In 1 Samuel 7:12, Samuel piled up stones as a monument to remind him that God had delivered the Philistines into his hand, and that Samuel and his men were victorious. He called the pile of stones *Ebenezer*, saying: "Thus far the Lord has helped us."

To me, an Ebenezer is things we do not want to forget. I learned a valuable lesson back in May of 1988, and thus far, I have not forgotten what God has done.

God is an amazing God. Every motor, bearing, rubber belt and every piece of wire had been burned up along with our roof. The employees helped me tear down and clean everything up. Local businesses helped us get new motors, bearings, belts and re-wire the whole manufacturing area. Within ten days, we were back in operation.

It was a miracle. But it didn't stop there.

We didn't replace the roof until late August. We operated with no roof, and only once did it rain during those times. We lost only half a day of production because of rain. The year 1988 ended up being a drought year, but that was a blessing for us.

Further, our finished goods warehouse did not burn. This meant we had enough product that we never missed an order during the time we worked to get back up and running.

"Thus far the Lord has helped us." 1 Samuel 7:12 (NIV)

I hope my fire story inspires you. It was one of the most impactful events of my life. It shifted me from being the provider to letting God be the provider. Consider the lessons here.

Have you been striving to be the provider? It isn't your place to be the provider. That is God's job. In our eagerness to achieve, somehow we take God's responsibility to provide and make it man's responsibility.

We need to repent for that.

**Prayer:**

Lord, I declare you are *Jehovah-Jireh*. You will provide for us. I repent for trying to take your job of providing, and for the times I have tried to make provision. Please forgive me. Help me to always remember that you are the provider, and that you are a good provider. Amen.

# 4

# Steward

CHRISTIANS HEAR MANY SERMONS on stewardship. I don't claim to know more than anyone else, but I have a unique perspective on stewarding. Having explained that God owns everything and that it is his responsibility to provide, I want to dive into the definition of a "Good Steward." How does a good steward look and act?

Let's look at the scripture commonly used to teach stewardship.

> *Again, it will be like a man going on a journey, who called his servants and entrusted his wealth to them. To one he gave five bags of gold, to another two bags, and to another one bag, each according to his ability.*
>
> Matthew 25:14

The first thing to notice is the word *entrusted.* Remember the definition for stewardship: "responsible management of something *entrusted* to one's care."

So, the man is asking these servants to *steward* his wealth. He is telling them to take good care of his money, which, incidentally, is not their money. He's a wealthy man who wants to go on vacation, so he has some workers take care of his money while he is gone.

When I first heard this story as a child, I pictured some rich guy randomly handing out his money to strangers and asking them to care for it. This was my first fallacy. This scripture says, "each according to their ability." These servants were unique in that they had the ability to handle money. Today, I picture these three men as part of the rich man's executive staff. They were probably in his accounting and investment office. They had a track record of making the wealthy man money. Clearly, he knew their abilities.

If I were going on vacation for a while, I would hand my money over to my top three investment people. I would give the five bags of gold to the person who had produced the most. I would give two bags to the next best, and one bag to the third best investment producer.

In studying this scripture, I researched how much a bag of gold was worth to these people. It came to twenty years' wages for a laborer. The 2025 average yearly income for a laborer is $46,000. In 20 years, that equals $920,000. Let's round up to $1MM per bag of gold. (What's $80,000 between friends?) So, in today's dollars, the servant entrusted with five bags of gold had $5MM to steward. The servant with two bags of gold had $2MM, and the servant with one bag had $1MM to steward. (Note: The designation "MM" stands for million.)

> *The man who had received five bags of gold went at once and put his money to work and gained five bags more. So also, the one with two bags of gold gained two more. But the man who had received one bag went off, dug a hole in the ground and hid his master's money.*
>
> Matthew 25:16-18

All told, the wealthy man passed out $8MM.

If someone handed you $5MM and said: "Invest it and grow it," would you know how?

What did they do with the money in Jesus' time? I doubt there was a stock market. I imagine they invested in commodities like grain, vegetables, and livestock. Maybe they opened a used camel dealership. "This creampuff was only ridden on Sundays by a little old lady from Bethlehem." Maybe they bought property and flipped it. Maybe they were the first "Fixer Upper" before Chip and Joanna Gaines. Maybe they built a strip mall with a Scrolls-A-Million, Eve's Apple Pies, and Noah's Boat Supply. We really have no idea how or what they did with the money, but the stakes were high.

> *After a long time the master of those servants returned and settled accounts with them. The man who had received five bags of gold brought the other five. 'Master,' he said, 'you entrusted me with five bags of gold. See, I have gained five more.'*
>
> *"His master replied, 'Well done, good and faithful servant! You have been faithful with a few things; I will put you in charge of many things. Come and share your master's happiness!'*
>
> Matthew 25:19-21

So, the wealthy guy returns from his extended winter along the Nile River, and the first investor brings him the original five million plus an additional five million. Nice!

Now, if I went away for the winter and I came back to find my money had doubled, I would be ecstatic as well. The master exclaimed, "Well done, good and faithful servant." I think all of us long to hear, "Well done, good and faithful servant." We love to be valued and appreciated. When our boss says "great job" on that project. Or "You are such a great asset to the company," it makes us feel warm and fuzzy all over. That servant felt pretty good at that moment.

The master went on to say: "You have been faithful with a few things; I will put you in charge of many things." Notice the principle at work. When we steward God's resources well, we get more to steward. I have seen this time and time again. When we are faithful with what we have to steward, we see an increase in what we steward next.

### Timing Is Everything

Another fallacy I had about this scripture started when I was young and stayed with me into my early adulthood. I imagined the day I passed away, standing before Heavenly Father at the pearly gates with my head down, fingers crossed, hoping and praying I get into heaven. And God says, "Well done, good and faithful servant. You have been faithful with little. I will put you in charge of much."

Now, I pictured this occurring at the end of my human life. And while it may happen this way, that is not what this scripture is describing. Far from a final, eternal reward, this interaction between the master and the servants occurred in the midst of their earthly lives. Consider: If we are dead, how can the master give us more to steward here on earth? The reward for a season of stewarding God's wealth is to hear God say, "Well done, good and faithful servant," and to receive more for the next season to steward.

So at the very least, God rewards us at the end of seasons in our lives. It happens more than we realize. It's how we grow. Yet more work is not the only reward.

### Celebrate Good Times

Notice the master's words: "Come share in your master's happiness." There was a cause for celebration.

Do you think if you had five million dollars and you made the master five million dollars more, he would just shake your hand, hand you a $50 Outback gift card, and move on? No. It says, "Come share in your master's happiness." I'm thinking there was a party for you and your friends. Maybe even a first-class trip with the master to Hawaii. It was a celebration, not just a thank you.

Of course, the rewards were in proportion to the gain.

*The man with two bags of gold also came. "Master," he said, "you entrusted me with two bags of gold; see, I have gained two more."*

*His master replied, "Well done, good and faithful servant! You have been faithful with a few things; I will put you in charge of many things. Come and share your master's happiness!"*

*Then the man who had received one bag of gold came. "Master," he said, "I knew that you are a hard man, harvesting where you have not sown and gathering where you have not scattered seed. So I was afraid and went out and hid your gold in the ground. See, here is what belongs to you."*

*His master replied, "You wicked, lazy servant! So you knew that I harvest where I have not sown and gather where I have not scattered seed? Well then, you should have put my money on deposit with the bankers, so that when I returned I would have received it back with interest.*

*"So take the bag of gold from him and give it to the one who has ten bags. For whoever has will be given more, and they will have an abundance. Whoever does not have, even what they have will be taken from them. And throw that worthless servant outside, into the darkness, where there will be weeping and gnashing of teeth."*

Matthew 25:22-28

We see that the steward with two bags of gold doubled his to four bags of gold, and the master was well pleased with this. But when the steward with one bag of gold returned just the original bag of gold, the master was angry. Remember, this servant was chosen according to his ability. He knew how to handle money. But he was lazy. He only performed when the master was watching. The master was so upset that he called him worthless and punished him for his disobedience by casting him out into the darkness, where there is weeping and gnashing of teeth. (Not exactly the Hawaiian vacation he was expecting.)

So, is this the master who, just a few verses earlier, was well pleased and celebrated with the two servants who had gained wealth? Yes, it is. Was the master Dr. Jekyll and Mr. Hyde? No, I don't think so. This master gave specific instructions on what the three were to do, but one decided to do his own thing. He was lazy, self-indulgent. As the master said, the least he could have done was to have put the gold in the bank, which would have made some interest.

This master was like any of us in the sense that we have different demeanors when faced with different circumstances. When my daughters were young, I tried to be a fun-loving dad. I played with them, took care of them, read stories at bedtime, prayed with them. I was a rather pleasant dad. But when they disobeyed, they saw a different dad—one who was stern and disciplined them. Same dad, but two different responses.

Allow me to tell you of something that changed my perspective on stewardship.

**Tough Times, God Times**

In 2014, our company, A Plus Powder Coaters, Inc, was finally taking off. We had 26 employees and 40,000 square feet of building. Sales were through the roof, and our buildings were packed with product to run. We needed more room and more equipment to handle the work. Laurie and I started praying and fasting about whether we should add on and build some new equipment. We felt God said yes, so I ordered a twenty-thousand-square-foot building, a state-of-the-art media blast room, a new powder-coating system, two forklifts, and two fifty-horse air compressors. Over the course of eleven months, we spent a lot of money in the way of capital investment.

We started construction in November 2014 and finished in March 2015. At that point, I installed the new blast system and air compressors. When that was finished, we moved the old blast system to the new building and added a new dust collector to this system. When finished, we moved on to the new batch powder-coating system.

One thing you need to know is that I am a mechanically oriented, hands-on guy. As such, I was my own general contractor for the new twenty-thousand-square-foot warehouse. I also designed the media blast booth and new powder system. I even helped install all the new equipment. Now, I did not merely supervise it; I was hands-on, bolting and welding things together. But because I was very busy during the eight months of 2015, I did not pay close attention to the business during that time. (Hey, I was having fun!)

Toward the end of that time, I noticed that we didn't seem as busy as we had been the previous year, but I had no idea how much we had slowed down until the installation of the new equipment was complete in September of 2015. As I examined the sales ledger, I realized we had gone from being very profitable to just breaking even. (For those not in business, breakeven is the point where you have enough sales or income to pay your bills, your employees and the raw material you need to operate, but you are not making a profit.)

When we started the expansion project, we had a fair amount of cash in the bank, so we were able to pay cash for the building project. We also had enough to pay for some of the equipment, but not all of it, so we used our line of credit from the bank.

Now, you may not be aware of this, but banks want to be paid back for the money they loan. The bank we borrowed from was no exception. Starting that September, they wanted monthly payments—something we couldn't do because we were operating at breakeven.

This weighed heavily on me, so I scraped together enough for the September payment. In October, things changed. We went from breakeven to losing money that month. This really stressed me. I started wondering if I had heard God correctly. Thoughts of possibly losing the company crossed my mind. That was scary.

Meanwhile, Laurie and I had been invited to Heartland Apostolic Prayer Network (HAPN) for their conference in October. The conference was coming up fast and my focus was on the survival of the business. Laurie and I decided to go, but I was torn. I felt guilty leaving our baby, A+, who was fighting for its life in the emergency room, surrounded by doctors shaking their heads as the machines were going BLEEP… BLEEP… BLEEP and getting slower and slower. Shouldn't I be helping with CPR?

The conference started on a Wednesday night. I don't remember who spoke, but I do remember they had us all come down front for prayer. When the prayer was over, they dismissed us. As I walked back to my seat, there stood Nancy Foreit, someone I knew from California. Nancy had spoken at the church we attend and had stayed in our home. She knew of me and our business and asked how I was doing.

Of course, I did what any good Christian would do. I lied.

"I'm doing great," I said, smiling.

Then she asked how business was. Oh, that hit a nerve. I unloaded with, "We are losing money and the bank wants to be paid. I am faced with possibly laying people off in a week, and it is almost the holiday season. What kind of shmuck does that? I don't want to be that guy."

The whole time I blabbed on, Nancy just stood there and smiled. When I was done, she said, "Bob, you just need to give it to the Lord."

It was all I could do to keep my eyes from rolling to the back of my head. I knew all that: *Lay it on the altar. God will take care of it. Blah blah blah.*

"Bob, I am a single, elderly woman on a limited income," she continued. "I gave my house to God. It is no longer mine. When my refrigerator broke, I prayed, 'Father God, your house has a broken refrigerator. What are you going to do about it?' God provided for the refrigerator to be fixed.

"Bob, when the roof started leaking, I didn't have the money for a new roof, so I prayed, 'Father God, your house has a leaky roof. What are you going to do about it?' And God provided a new roof."

Bells and whistles were going off in my head like a winning jackpot in a casino. She was talking about stewardship—the careful, responsible management of something entrusted to one's care.

That evening, as we drove to our hotel, I told Laurie about my new revelation of stewardship. We went to bed around 11:00. I dozed lightly and woke up thinking about stewardship. I finally got up somewhere around 12:30 and sat on the couch. I asked God to forgive me for trying to be the owner and provider. I repented for my attitude and actions.

For the last month or so, I felt a heavy pressure on my chest to provide for my employees. I felt heavy pressure on my shoulders to pay the bank. As I repented, the weight on my chest and shoulders lifted. I could breathe easier. I had stepped into a new dimension of stewardship.

With my new revelation, I started praying differently.

"Father God, I remind you that A+ is yours, not mine; that it is your responsibility to provide for A+. As your steward, what do you have for me to do? Help me stay in my lane. Father, if A+ is supposed to close, help me do it by walking uprightly like a man of God."

Thank God, we didn't have to close the business.

Of course, I would love to tell you that in the next few weeks, things turned around dramatically, but they didn't. Sales continued to drop. We were losing large amounts of money, but I was a new man.

My wife and close friends can attest to the changes. Prior to my encounter with Nancy, I could maintain my composure while at work, but when I got home, I took it out on the one I loved the most—my wife, Laurie. She couldn't even ask how my day was without me snapping at her. I was working every waking moment before the change, but after the revelation of God's ownership, I went back to ten-hour days. I came home in the evening, had dinner with Laurie, and played cards or watched TV with her.

Our good friends, Mark and Sheri, have known me since I was a freshman in high school. We built a house next to them and raised our children together. At the time, we would go out to dinner at least once a week and play cards afterwards. My point being: they knew me. We had been out to dinner one night, and as we played cards, I told them about my newfound revelation about stewardship.

Sheri said, "Bob, we have known each other most of our lives. I could always tell when you are stressed or had an issue at A+ because you become withdrawn, quiet and don't make us laugh. But had you not told me A+ was struggling, I would have never known. This stewardship thing must be working."

A Plus Powder Coaters struggled and continued to lose money until about February 2016. Then God opened the floodgates, and we became profitable again. We were able to pay all our bank loans off quickly.

The night in the hotel, when I prayed and asked forgiveness, it was a monumental moment in my life. I did not want to forget what God had shown me. I wanted a way to remember my stewardship revelation, so I wrote a declaration that I could frame and hang on the wall to remind me of stewardship. As I finished writing it and was about to email it to the printer in town, I looked up the word *declaration*. It means, "a loud firm voice." Well, I wanted that, but then I looked up *decree*. "A legally binding document." That was what I wanted. You see, Robert Henderson had been to our church and spoke on the Courts of Heaven, and I wanted a legally binding document between my Father God and me. I wanted another Ebenezer monument—something to help me remember what God had taught me.

**Decree of Ownership (Business Decree)**

> I, Robert & Laurie Bertelsen, current owners of A Plus Powder Coaters, Inc., on this date, 12/5/15, give the aforementioned company, including but not limited to the land, buildings, equipment, contents and all other assets, to the Lord God. From this time forward, it will be 100% the Lord's. I relinquish my ownership and trade my ownership for stewardship. I pledge to be the best steward of what God has entrusted to me. I acknowledge that I am an ambassador for him wherever I represent this company. I will not try to regain control of the company but will work diligently to follow the Lord's vision for the company from this day forth.

I have this decree framed and hanging in my office by the door, so I see it every time I leave my office. I have since written a separate decree for our home. Laurie and I have one signed and hanging in our den. I have also made one for ministries. The decrees can be purchased at www.finishlineresources.com/.

It has been more than ten years since I had this revelation of stewardship. A+ has grown from twenty-six employees to eighty employees. We have been debt-free since we paid off the line of credit in 2016. I still use the prayer strategy I used in 2015 when I had the revelation. For instance, when I am looking for management positions, I pray, "Father, your business needs this management position filled. What are you going to do?"

Another example. "Lord, your company has an issue with a supplier. What are you going to do about it?"

When I have a customer who won't pay their bill: "Father, your business has a customer who won't pay. I leave it in your hands, as it is your company and your money."

When I don't know what to do: "Father, I remind myself that A+ is yours and not mine. Help me to know what your plan is for…."

When I remind God, I am really reminding myself that the business is his. I don't think God is forgetful.

**Prayer**

Father God, I repent for not stewarding what you have entrusted to me. I ask you to help me change my perspective from owner to steward. Help me to pray and operate from stewardship, not ownership. Amen!

# Part II

# Actions

*Faith, Work, Increase*

# 5

# Faith

HAVING ESTABLISHED THE THREE MINDSETS of a good steward, we will now examine the three actions of a good steward—the things we need to do. Stewardship, it turns out, is a verb. Far from lying around waiting, hoping or praying for a financial increase to fall into our laps, it requires activity on our part.

Let's look at three specific actions of the stewards from Matthew 25.

**Faith**

The first action they had was faith. Personally, I believe *faith* is misspelled. It should be spelled *R-I-S-K.* Yes, *risk.* Because you cannot have faith without taking a risk. Allow me to explain.

It takes no faith for me to stand up and walk. I've done it millions of times in my life, although my early attempts were shaky. However, it would take great faith for me to believe I could walk on water. It isn't the normal thing for me to do. So, if I say, "I believe I can walk on water," and it doesn't happen, the risk is that I could drown, or worse: I could look really foolish. So, if something is a sure thing, there is no risk, thus no faith is involved.

Now, the risk can be physical, emotional, or spiritual. For example, I can believe that the lame person I am praying for will stand up and walk. The risk for me is failure and all that comes with it: being embarrassed, losing my reputation, and disappointing the person eager to stand.

Likewise, if I jump from an airplane without a parachute, declaring God will save me, if God doesn't save me, I not only look foolish, but life could come to an abrupt conclusion. (It's not the fall that kills you. It's the sudden stop at the end.)

### Five Bags of Gold

> *The man who had received five bags of gold went at once and put his money to work and gained five bags more.*
>
> Matthew 25:16

From chapter 3, recall that the present-day value of 5 bags of gold comes to $5MM. (MM stands for "million.") That is a lot of money. The thought of doubling it in a short time would be intimidating, requiring a significant risk. The scripture does not give us a timeline for when the master returned, but I think it is safe to assume a few years. This steward with 5 bags of gold had to take a risk to double his money in a relatively short amount of time. He didn't just throw money at any old thing. He must have been wise about it. And certainly, there were ups and downs. Investments rarely rise seamlessly; more of a sawtooth climb. Such is the walk of faith.

### Powder Coaters in Faith

In faith, I started A Plus Powder Coaters, Inc. I had no previous experience in powder-coating, and I knew nothing about the technology involved. Still, I believed God told me to do it, so I stepped out in faith and started the business. I believed it could work. The risk was that I could lose all the money I invested, including the money I borrowed and my house that I mortgaged. If A+ didn't make it, I would be in dire straits. The risk was far more than just looking foolish; it was losing everything I owned.

When Laurie and I were praying about whether or not to start a powder-coating business, I told her, "We could lose everything we have except for two things. Our relationship with God, and our marriage." Then I added: "If I need to, I'll pump gas."

Which was a hollow promise since gas stations promptly went to self-serve. *Gee, God. Talk about burning our boats on the shore!* Thankfully, God came through, and A+ is still going strong.

**Calculated Risks**

As stewards, we need faith and the ability to take risks. I am not condoning throwing money at everything that comes your way. That would not be wise. But you sometimes need to take calculated risks to grow the resources God has given you. For instance, if you are getting 0.25% on your savings account, you could put it to work 4% or 5% in a money fund. It's a little reward for little risk, but at least you are earning something. But if you are really going to grow what God has entrusted to us to steward, you need to take bigger risks. Perhaps the stock market. Even riskier: the commodities market. (Don't do that.)

There is nothing wrong with asking God for wisdom and the ability to take more risk. I know some people who are very conservative, and others who can easily take big risks. The question is: What level of faith is God calling you to? Is it to take more risk? Or less? My tolerance for risk might not be your level of tolerance. Again, we need to consult God and listen for him to speak.

Growing faith is a stretch for all of us.

If it wasn't, it really wouldn't be faith.

**Prayer**

Father God, I ask forgiveness for not exercising my faith and not taking risks. Would you help me step out in faith when you are calling me to? Help me not fear risks, but embrace them when you are leading me to take risk and operate in faith. I pray I become more comfortable working in faith and taking risks. Amen!

# 6

# Work

THE SECOND ACTION a steward must take is work. *What, I have to work?* Yes! As we look at the two good stewards, we see that they worked.

> *The man who had received five bags of gold went at once and put his money to work and gained five more.*
>
> Matt. 25:16

Again, five bags of gold here represent $5MM in today's money.

Now, do you think the good steward who had five bags to steward lounged on their cushions, tossed grapes into their mouth, and waited for the five million to double on its own? Of course not. They had to work to double the money.

We can only speculate how the good steward doubled his money. He possibly bought land and developed it. Or he might have bought livestock and sold them or built a housing development. We don't know, but what I do know is you don't double five million bucks by doing nothing. You have to work.

**The Lord Loves A Working Man**

Do you realize work is one of the first things God spoke about in the Old Testament? From Genesis 2:15:

> *The Lord God took the man and put him in the Garden of Eden to work it and take care of it.*

*Wait, Adam had to work?* Yes, he did. He was placed in the garden to work it and to take care of it. We often think that Adam and Eve had a great life, running around naked, getting great tans, and eating whatever they wanted. But this scripture says they had to work. They had a garden to tend, bushes to trim, tree limbs to gather, soil to till, vines to prune, a harvest to gather…and snakes to repel.

Not only did they care for the garden, but they were also told to name all the animals.

> *So the man gave names to all the livestock, the birds in the sky and all the wild animals.*
>
> Genesis 2: 20

So you can add "animal husbandry" to their list of responsibilities. Think about how big a job this must have been. How many animals are there, anyway? A few hundred would not be a big deal. But according to Ourworldindata.org, there are:

- 6,596 Mammals
- 11,188 Birds
- 11,733 Reptiles
- 36,367 Fishes
- 1,050,000 Insects
- 1,175,134 Total

Eve: "How was your day, dear? What did you do?"

Adam: "Oh, I named 255 animals today.

Eve: "You did over 300 yesterday."

Adam: "Do you have any idea how hard it is to come up with new names? I already named the easy ones: cow, dog, cat, fox, Bob. Now I'm up to elephants, kangaroos and rhinoceros. And I don't get me started on the duck-billed platypus!"

Eve: "Yes, dear, I know. And just wait until you finally get to the: parastratiosphecomyia stratiosphecomyioide."

Perhaps this is why we are told:

> *Never be lazy, but work hard and serve the Lord enthusiastically.*
>
> Romans 12:11 NLT

We are commanded to work hard and serve the Lord with enthusiasm. This reads like working hard and serving the Lord are tied together. Are we to be enthusiastic about our work and about God? I'm thinking we should be.

Also, notice the admonishment: "Never be *lazy.*" Defined as: "unwilling to work or use energy."

We also see a reference to laziness in Matthew 25:26:

> *His master replied, "You wicked, lazy servant! So you knew that I harvest where I have not sown and gather where I have not scattered seed?"*

And in verse 30, we read the consequences for laziness:

> *"And throw that worthless servant outside, into the darkness, where there will be weeping and gnashing of teeth."*

To say the master does not tolerate lazy servants would be an understatement. He calls them *worthless*. That is pretty harsh. I think I would choose working hard over being lazy, worthless, and getting tossed into a place of darkness, weeping and gnashing of teeth.

Ephesians 6:7 tells us:

> *Work with enthusiasm, as though you were working for the Lord rather than for people. (NLT)*

Our call is not work for work's sake. Rather, we need to remember we are working for the Lord. We should have a good attitude about it.

*Whatever you do, work at it with all your heart, as working for the Lord, not for human masters, since you know that you will receive an inheritance from the Lord as a reward. It is the Lord Christ you are serving.*

Colossians 3:23-24

**Work In Action**

At A Plus Powder Coaters, Inc., I have worked over the years to grow the employees from just me to over 80 employees. Over the last 13 years, I have been intentional about working on our culture and valuing our co-workers, making sure they know they are our greatest asset.

I have also worked on growing the physical size of the buildings. When we started in 1996, we had 11,250 square feet. Today we are at 115,000 square feet—an order of magnitude in growth. (I imagine by the time this book goes to print, it will even be greater.)

More than buildings, however, I am focused on growing people. I have heard from young people saying they hope to be where I am one day. What they see, however, is a successful steward of a company, a guy who has a nice home, several cars (including some old muscle cars and Corvettes), and the ability to travel frequently. From what they see, I have the perfect life.

Well…I do, but they don't see the sacrifice, long hours, prayer life and my personal struggles. And what they never seem to ever ask is, "How did you get here?"

I didn't start out where I am today. In fact, when we got married, our annual income was $14,000. We were not taking expensive vacations. We seldom went out to dinner. We were happy just to have basic food on the table.

*Oh? Cheerios Fricassee again? Maybe I'll just eat the box.*

I worked long, hard hours for many years. As an employee, I volunteered for all the overtime I could get. Laurie and I cut firewood on the weekends and sold it to pay our heating bill. I took any odd job I could find. When I had the opportunity to buy our first business, I had a choice: *Which half of the day did I want to work?*

When we started A Plus Powder Coaters Inc in 1996, I worked from 6 am to 9 pm Monday through Friday, 6 am to 5 pm on Saturday. I took Sundays off to honor God and my family. I am fortunate today to be semi-retired (by my standards) and working 7 am to 5 pm, Monday through Friday, and an occasional Saturday. I average about fifty hours per week when I am in town.

I do take a fair amount of time off to travel and speak at conferences and churches. My point is that people who want to be where I am today need to consider the work that it takes to both get there and stay there. (With regard to "stay there," the fact is, there is no such thing as standing still in business. If you are not advancing, the market will advance without you and you'll be left behind.)

Some want the reward without the work. And yet, work is one of the things we are called of God to do. Truth be told: work is its own reward.

> *If you are a thief, quit stealing. Instead, use your hands for good hard work, and then give generously to others in need.*
>
> Ephesians 4:28 NLT
>
> *Work willingly at whatever you do, as though you were working for the Lord rather than for people.*
>
> Colossians 3:23 NLT

As Christians, the Lord will give you an inheritance as your reward. The Master you are serving is Christ. When we work, we are working for Christ. We are fulfilling our responsibility. We are called to work. We need to shift from thinking: *I work for XYZ company* and start thinking: *Although I work for that company, I am really working for the Lord. He is my provider, and I work for him, not the company.*

> *Even while we were with you, we gave you this command: "Those unwilling to work will not get to eat." Yet we hear that some of you are living idle lives, refusing to work and meddling in other people's business. We command such people and urge them in the name of the Lord Jesus Christ to settle down and work to earn their own living.*
>
> 2 Thessalonians 3:10-12 NLT

I find this scripture interesting.

Paul is saying: If you are unwilling to work, then you shouldn't eat. He is not talking about fasting (although it might do some good). He is saying you don't deserve to eat. Now, the context was that able-bodied believers who were unwilling to work should not be supported by the Christian community. Yet the principle still applies today. If you won't work, your hunger is on you.

One slight word of caution. The command to work does not mean we are to be workaholics.

*But Bob, you said you worked a pile of hours when you first started A Plus Powder Coaters, Inc.*

I did, but in hindsight, it was because of my control issues that hadn't been dealt with at that point. Today, I'm a much different man. I get up early, spend an hour or two in prayer, then work until 5 pm, and come home to my lovely wife. Plus, I will come home early (4:30 pm!) if there is a compelling reason. Or I might even take an hour or two off to help at church.

My point being: There may be a season when you and your spouse agree that you should spend more time on the business, but it must be a season, not a permanent change.

Here is our challenge:

- Are you willing to work as a good steward?
- Are you willing to put in the hours and energy God has called you to do?

What God requires of me may be different than what he has called you to do. That's ok. Such is the beauty of our heavenly Father. He has an individual plan for each of us.

Our common ground is this: As good stewards, we are all called to work. So work, we shall!

**Prayer**

Lord, I pray you would forgive me for anytime I have been lazy. Help me to work and do my best and not be lazy. I understand work is something you created me for, and I want to fulfill my role and work diligently towards the things you have called me to do. Amen!

# 7

# Increase

GOOD STEWARDS BRING INCREASE. When I say *increase*, I mean "increasing the value and the size of the amount." This action is two-fold: we bring increase, and God brings increase. We know that the man who had received five bags of gold brought the other five.

> *"Master," he said, "you entrusted me with five bags of gold. See, I have gained five more."*
>
> Matthew 25:20

The job of bringing increase is pretty clear in this scripture. The good steward doubled what he had been entrusted with. Five bags of gold turned into 10 bags of gold. Simple math says he increased the five bags by five more for a total of ten bags.

So, what do I mean by God bringing increase? Consider:

> *So take the bag of gold from him and give it to the one who has ten bags.*
>
> *For whoever has will be given more, and they will have an abundance.*
>
> Matthew 25:28-29

The master took the bag of gold from the lazy steward with one bag of gold, and he gave it to the good steward who already had ten bags of gold. Hence, the master gave an additional increase to the top-performing steward. Likewise, God, our master, also gives us increase. We make increase and God gives increase. Paul wrote:

> *Now he who supplies seed to the sower and bread for food will also supply and increase your store of seed and will enlarge the harvest of your righteousness.*
>
> 2 Corinthians 9:10

God increases the seed and the harvest.

> *May the Lord give you increase, you and your children! May you be blessed by the Lord, who made heaven and earth!*
>
> Psalm 115:14-15 ESV

God gives us increase. I don't know about you, but I want God's increase. I love that it is generational—an increase for my children and me. How awesome is that?

> *Honor the Lord with your wealth and with the best part of everything you produce.*
>
> *Then he will fill your barns with grain, and your vats will overflow with good wine.*
>
> Proverbs 3:9-10 NLT

Here God goes again, bringing increase. Not just a little, but overflowing. That's the kind of increase I want to see in my finances.

One of the things we are constantly working on at A Plus Powder Coaters, Inc., is increasing sales. The abiding principle is that no matter how busy or big a business gets, we should never quit trying to grow. We set yearly goals for acquiring new customers. For a business as well-established as we are, it is becoming difficult to find new customers. But my salesman beats the pavement daily, trying to increase our customer base. Terry is very good at it.

With increased sales, we can increase our employees, which means we can benefit more people's lives. Still, the final increase we work for is profitability. I want to see our profitability increase.

I believe God is in all three of these areas: customers, profit, and employees. He has brought us many customers in numerous ways. Some were reached by our sales team. Others saw our website and admired our culture. (We are not shy about our reliance on God.) And God has brought us some great co-workers. Some heard we are a Christian-run company and applied. Some came because of the testimonies of our current employees. God brings great employees to us. I have had several employees tell me they saw our website, that we are a Christian company, and they wanted to work here.

All of this has also increased our profitability. As of this writing, we are having a record-breaking year. We are at numbers I never dreamed of. The cash flow has been amazing to watch. God has been so good to us. This increase in cash has enabled us to add 17,000 square feet this year without borrowing any money. It has also supplied some new equipment we wanted. I must say, God is a great provider and brings increase at the right time.

**Practical Considerations**

Are you working on bringing an increase to your finances? You may not own a business, but there are things you can do to bring an increase. Do you have a mortgage on your home? Do you realize it is part of your net worth?

I spoke at a conference a couple of months ago. I read the definition of a millionaire. "An individual whose net worth—total assets minus total liabilities—is equal to or exceeds one million units of currency."

So, what is an asset? It is something that has value and generally increases in value. For instance, a house typically increases in value. (At least, in a good market.)

Liabilities, on the other hand, are things that depreciate in value. Consider a car. You buy a new car for $50,000, and when it is paid off in five years, it's worth $20,000. That is a liability, as it lost value. (Although you got a lot of great miles from it.)

You see, our perspective of a millionaire is someone with a million dollars of cash. That is not the correct definition. A millionaire is someone whose net worth is $1MM or greater. Net worth is our assets minus our liabilities.

When I explain this to people, they do a quick calculation in their minds and sometimes realize they are millionaires. Their house has appreciated significantly, perhaps they have a 401K account, maybe some stocks have done well, and those depreciating cars are still worth something. Taking into account the value of all they own, they subtract any debt (total liability of their mortgage, car payments, school loans, alimony, or child support), and it turns out, their net worth is greater than $1MM.

This means our goal in increasing wealth is to increase our net worth.

Here's a quick way to increase your net worth. Pay off your house early. It's easier than you might think. Consider paying extra on the principal of your home loan. (Most house payments are more interest than principal.) If you made one extra payment to your principal per year, it could shorten a thirty-year loan by seven years. Likewise, paying $100 extra towards the principal on the average mortgage could save over $65,000 in interest over the life of the loan.

Other ways to bring an increase are a budget. A budget is a good tool, but we can't become dogmatic about it. There are times when God may call us to deviate from our budget and trust Him. That being said, a budget can eliminate frivolous spending and free up cash to make extra mortgage payments or be able to invest to grow the wealth you are stewarding. Increase is a matter of discipline, which is another form of work.

**Prayer**

Lord, I ask forgiveness for not being intentional in bringing increase to the things you have entrusted to me. I pray you would lead me, teach me and show me how I can bring increase to the things you have called me to steward. Amen!

# 8
# Actions at Work In The Bible

HAVING EXAMINED FAITH, WORK AND INCREASE, let's examine financial increase and see how these actions apply to it.

Over the years, I have heard many speakers talk about the transfer of wealth, as when God transfers wealth to someone. Here's an example of this. Let's see how the three actions of a steward played a role.

**Poor to Oil Tycoon**

Here is a story from the life of Elisha, the prophet who succeeded Elijah.

*****

*The wife of a man from the company of the prophets cried out to Elisha, "Your servant my husband is dead, and you know that he revered the Lord. But now his creditor is coming to take my two boys as his slaves."*

*Elisha replied to her, "How can I help you? Tell me, what do you have in your house?"*

*"Your servant has nothing there at all," she said, "except a small jar of olive oil."*

*Elisha said, "Go around and ask all your neighbors for empty jars. Don't ask for just a few. Then go inside and shut*

> *the door behind you and your sons. Pour oil into all the jars, and as each is filled, put it to one side."*
>
> *She left him and shut the door behind her and her sons. They brought the jars to her and she kept pouring. When all the jars were full, she said to her son, "Bring me another one." But he replied, "There is not a jar left." Then the oil stopped flowing.*
>
> *She went and told the man of God, and he said, "Go, sell the oil and pay your debts. You and your sons can live on what is left."*
>
> 2 Kings 4:1-7

This woman went from being poor and almost losing her children to being an oil tycoon. Can you relate? If someone were coming to take your children, wouldn't you sell anything you could to prevent it? Mortgage the house. Beg, borrow and steal anything you could. The debt must have been quite large that this widow couldn't just refinance her house or borrow from friends and family to pay off the debtors.

Look at the steps God required of her.

Faith

First, she had to take a risk and ask her neighbors for jars. Lots of jars. Remember, the prophet said, "Don't just ask for a few."

Now, consider: What kind of risk is it to ask your neighbors for something? Have you ever been cooking and run out of a key ingredient? You don't have time to run to the store, so you ask your neighbor for a couple of eggs, a cup of flour, or a rack of lamb. And what is the first thing they ask you? *What are you making?*

This woman was sent to the neighbors to ask for jars. What do you suppose they asked her?

"Oh? You want to borrow every container I have? What are you going to do with all these jars?"

"The prophet told me to get all these jars so I can pay my bills."

"How in the world is collecting jars going to pay your bills?"

Yeah…if this doesn't work, you are going to look pretty foolish. That's the risk sometimes. None of us ever wants to be ashamed. Today, we would just order one hundred containers from Amazon and stand guard against porch pirates. That way, no one could make fun of us if it didn't work. *Oh, how spoiled we are.* Yet the widow had faith and took a risk to get a bunch of jars.

Work

Second, she had to work to collect the jars. They didn't just show up on her porch. She had to walk to the neighbors' houses and carry the jars back to her house. She would have made a lot of trips to do this. Maybe not the hardest work in the world, but it still constitutes effort.

Increase

Lastly, she saw God's increase. She had enough oil to pay the debtors and still live on. She had a large increase.

**From Slave to Wealthy Elite**

Here's what the Israelites did when preparing for the exodus.

> *And the people of Israel did as Moses had instructed; they asked the Egyptians for clothing and articles of silver and gold. The Lord caused the Egyptians to look favorably on the Israelites, and they gave the Israelites whatever they asked for. So they stripped the Egyptians of their wealth!*
>
> Exodus 12:35-36 NLT

Now, in this action, there was a very high risk involved. The Israelites were slaves. Slaves got beaten just for asking for a break, a drink or food. Some would even have been killed for doing lesser things than asking for their master's disposable wealth. Yet the Israelites had strong faith in taking such a big risk.

A typical slave worked for years with no reward except the privilege of living to work another day. And we complain about our lives when the air conditioning quits or the heat stops working. *We have it so bad!* They worked as slaves their whole lives, making bricks for the Egyptians.

We should take notice. God is our provider. Yet we sometimes think we should be paid more for our labor. We need to look past our paycheck and allow God to provide. If we work hard, God will provide the desired increase. It might not look like a paycheck, but we will get what God feels we deserve.

The increase realized from the Egyptians was huge. They got all the gold, silver, Gucci, Prada, Louis Vuitton clothing they wanted. (I have it on good authority that a classic chariot was included, too.) They even had enough to build a golden calf. (Not their best decision.) I envision a full-scale calf, which would take a lot of gold.

**Poor Shepherd to Wealthy King**

The shepherd David worked hard to contribute to his family. One day, he saw his opportunity for something greater.

> *Now the Israelites had been saying, "Do you see how this man keeps coming out? He comes out to defy Israel. The king will give great wealth to the man who kills him. He will also give him his daughter in marriage and will exempt his family from taxes in Israel."*
>
> 1 Samuel 17:25

Clearly, David took a big risk by going against Goliath. Whenever your life is on the line, risk is off the charts. Scholars say Goliath was 9 feet tall and weighed over 500 pounds. David was a young man, 13 or 14 years old. He was probably just over five feet tall and weighed 125 pounds, dripping wet. Now, if there was a fight between a nine-foot-tall, 500-pound giant and a diminutive teenager, we'd all put our money on the giant. The odds were stacked against David. Yet David had faith in God and charged Goliath.

Little did Goliath know that David was preparing for this moment since he was a lad. As the shepherd of the family sheep, part of that job was fending off predators. In his own words:

> *The Lord who rescued me from the paw of the lion and the paw of the bear will rescue me from the hand of this Philistine.*
>
> 1 Samuel 17:37

It turns out, David didn't start his fighting career against a giant. He worked his way up to it. He had killed lions and bears—no, not from Detroit or Chicago—before he met up with Goliath. Still, it's a safe assumption that when David faced his first bear or lion, they seemed like a giant to him. When he finally faced a real giant, those victories against wild animals boosted his confidence that he could prevail in his battle in the name of the Lord.

Of course, every battle is not against a giant, even though it may seem like it. Giant is a relative term. Yet every victory gives us that much more courage to face our next giants, even if they are from New York.

Think about the increase David received from God: great wealth from King Saul, a wife, and a tax exemption for his family. Now, the tax exemption alone would be enough for me to consider fighting the giant. (Or maybe I'd just challenge him to an auto race.)

Later in life, David gave of his personal treasures to the building of the temple, estimated to be twenty billion dollars. Clearly, he had done well with the reward he earned that day.

# Part III

# Characteristics

*Integrity, Trustworthiness, Generosity*

# 9

# Integrity

HAVING EXAMINED THE THREE ACTIONS of a good steward, let's now consider the three characteristics of a good steward. These are things I have not only seen in scripture but also experienced as modeled by people I believe to be good stewards.

**Integrity**

The first characteristic is integrity. According to the Oxford Language Dictionary:

> Integrity: "the quality of being honest and having strong moral principles; moral uprightness."

The words *honest* and *strong moral principles* jump out at me. The good stewards in Matthew 25 must have been of strong moral principles. It would have been so easy for them to do nothing, maybe spend a bag or two of gold on some slick racing camels or a vacation in Syria. And when the master returned, they'd just say their investments didn't do very well. That's what the worthless steward did. He hid it in the ground and sat at home watching Hebrew TV.

Integrity is doing the right thing when no one is looking. Do you live the same lifestyle you preach when no one is around? Integrity is tougher than some might think. Think about how many Christian leaders have preached sexual purity yet experienced adulterous affairs. They appear holy, righteous people of integrity, but in their secluded time, they lived by (or succumbed to) a different code.

The stewards in Matthew 25 appeared to have integrity, even the steward who buried the bag of gold. They had a great professional appearance, although two of them were real and one was a fake. The lazy steward talked a good line; in fact, he fooled the master into thinking he had integrity, so the master entrusted part of his wealth to him. But you can only fool someone part of the time. Eventually, our integrity (or lack thereof) reveals itself.

From his youth, Daniel was a person of integrity, as we see when Nebuchadnezzar, King of Babylon, captured Jerusalem.

> *"Then the king ordered Ashpenaz, chief of his court officials, to bring into the king's service some of the Israelites from the royal family and the nobility— young men without any physical defect, handsome, showing aptitude for every kind of learning, well informed, quick to understand, and qualified to serve in the king's palace. He was to teach them the language and literature of the Babylonians. The king assigned them a daily amount of food and wine from the king's table. They were to be trained for three years, and after that they were to enter the king's service."*
>
> Daniel 1:3-5

Daniel was one of the chosen youths. The plan was to indoctrinate/brainwash the youths into the Babylon culture. The first test of integrity came when the king told them to eat from his table. Daniel refused the king's food. Notice that he did not rationalize away his principles with excuses like, "What's the harm in great food and good wine?" When confronted with temptation, Daniel's integrity kicked in, and he flatly refused to partake.

Yet the King's food was merely the first test.

In Daniel 6, some government officials decide to flatter the king and ask him to make a law that no one can pray to any god or human except King Nebuchadnezzar, and if anyone doesn't comply, they will be thrown into the lions' den. I'm pretty sure they did this to eliminate Daniel. The king favored Daniel over the rest of the officials, and that made them jealous.

When Daniel heard of this law, he went home and prayed three times a day near an open window. Now, if he were not a man of integrity, he might have gone to the basement and prayed secretly.

The officials told the King that someone was praying to another god besides him. The king got mad and had the perpetrator brought before him. When he saw it was Daniel, he regretted his decision but had to follow through with the law he had passed. Daniel was thrown into the lions' den. As we all know, Daniel survived the ordeal. Turns out, the lions were vegan…at least for a day. The point being: Daniel was a man of demonstrated integrity, even when it could have cost him his life.

**Who's Watching?**

As good Christian stewards, we must have integrity. What do you do when no one is looking? Are you the same when you are at church as when you are at home? Good stewards are the same all the time, not just when the master is watching.

If you are in line at a store and a person drops a dollar bill, do you pick it up and return it to them? Or do you slide your foot over it and grab it when no one's looking? What if they dropped a stack of hundred-dollar bills? Would you still return it? Or justify keeping it? *Think of the tithe, God!*

Integrity is integrity, no matter the amount. A person of integrity would pick up the money and return it, with no thought of keeping it, no matter the amount. From Proverb 11:3 NKJV:

> *The integrity of the upright will guide them, But the perversity of the unfaithful will destroy them.*

Is integrity guiding you even in secret? If not, you will be destroyed. We need integrity to be our moral compass for God to give us increase.

Integrity is foundational in stewardship. A foundation is what a building is built upon. If the foundation is done right, the building will stand for a long time. If the foundation is faulty, the building will sink and eventually crumble and fall. Just like a foundation, integrity determines how long something will stand.

I teach on finances and stewardship. What I write and speak about, I also live, even when no one is looking. I must be a man of integrity, or eventually, the life I am building will fail.

A good steward must have integrity.

**Terry Watson**

Tim Dunsmore, who helped me build the equipment and start production in the early years of A+, ran the shop for me. He was one of my best friends at the time. I loved seeing Tim each day at work. Well, he ran the shop for a year, then he told me he was leaving. He wanted to move back to his home state of Michigan, plus he didn't feel being a supervisor was a good fit for him.

I was devastated. He was a vital part of building the equipment, establishing our capabilities, hiring shop employees, and supervising the day-to-day operation.

Tim recommended we hire Terry Watson. I knew of Terry. He had been raised in a bar by his grandmother, who owned the bar. He was a little rough around the edges. He had been in some trouble, but he eventually came to the Lord.

After praying about it, I felt Terry was the right person, so I invited him for an interview. I felt God had told me the wage to offer him. Terry arrived, we talked, and I made him the offer. He sat there quietly for a few moments, then said he would take the job. Later,

Terry told me he had prayed about the job, and if I offered him a certain amount or more, he would take it. The number I gave him was the number he had in mind.

He told me during the initial interview that if there was ever an opportunity in sales, he would like an opportunity there. At the time, I was doing all the sales. In 2000, we had not made enough to break even (the place where the income from sales is enough to pay all the bills and wages). I was desperate, so I decided to let Terry do sales two days a week, and I would run the shop on those two days. Long story short, he did an amazing job. I eventually put him in full-time sales.

Terry is a man of integrity. There have been times when he could have sacrificed his integrity and padded his pocket, or made a sale if only he would do away with his integrity. But that isn't Terry.

I trust Terry one hundred percent. He has grown to not only be my sales manager but also a close friend. His integrity is impeccable.

Case in point: Terry was trying to get the business from a potential customer. He presented the quote to the purchasing manager. The purchasing manager mentioned how they like seeing a cash kickback at the end of the year. Terry had to make a decision. He could take cash out of his commission on the sales and give it to this guy, or he could say, "I don't operate that way, neither does A+ operate that way." He chose the latter because of his integrity.

Another time, in the very early days when we were desperate to break even, a customer Terry called on had a large job. In fact, it would have equated to thirty percent of our monthly revenue. We were awarded the job. *Thank you, Jesus!* I ordered the powder we would need to fulfill the order, and Terry was told the parts to be powder-coated would show up on Monday of next week.

Well, the powder arrived, but no parts. After a day or so, Terry called the purchasing person. This person said his dad owned the company and that he (the son) was paid based on the highest and lowest quotes for powder-coating. They used the highest price in their quote to their customer, but awarded the work to the lowest quote.

We had been the lowest quote, but after he awarded us the work, another company came in cheaper. We could still have the work he promised us; however, if we just lowered our already low price. The purchasing person also told Terry that his pay was the difference between the high and low prices, so he would not move off the lowest price.

We needed that work badly, but when I looked at the numbers to run the production, we would lose money. We had to pass on the job.

A year later, Terry stopped by the company to see if they had any work we could quote. The doors were locked, and a sign over their company said, "Out of Business."

Their lack of integrity cost them their business.

As I said, I trust Terry's integrity. I don't question it or second-guess it. I know Terry is a man of integrity and will always do what is right.

We have heard of companies that, in order to give them a bid, you have to supply cash for them to even consider it. Where is their integrity? Are they looking out for the best interest of the company or themselves? Short-term gain? Or long-term growth?

Our integrity builds over time, but it only takes a moment to sacrifice it all. Yes, integrity can be rebuilt, but it takes time once it has been compromised.

Are you living a life of integrity? Do you need to make some changes and start being intentional about your integrity? Consider the following prayer.

**Prayer**

Lord God, I confess to making poor decisions based on immediate gain. I let the circumstances of the present need impact my honest relationship with others, and most importantly, my relationship with you. I repent of my poor choices and lack of integrity. I submit to you for rebuilding that which you want to instill in my character. Amen!

# 10

# Trustworthiness

TRUSTWORTHINESS IS VITAL to being a good steward. God has entrusted us with gifts and resources, and we need to be trustworthy stewards of them.

Trustworthy: "Able to be trusted."

The Cambridge Dictionary

Now, our first thought might be: *Aren't trustworthiness and integrity the same?* No, they are different, but they complement each other. Hard to have one without the other. Integrity is when I do something right, whether anyone is looking or not. This generally reflects my personal convictions regarding my own stuff. Trustworthy means I can be trusted with someone else's stuff.

### Trustworthiness in Courtship

My oldest daughter was in college, and a young man had an interest in her. He asked me for permission to date her. This was a process I instituted when my girls were in high school. They went to a small Christian school, and I told them that if someone asked them out, the young man had to ask my permission. I also told my girls that if they didn't want to go out with the person, just tell me, and when the young man asks permission to date them, I'll tell him no.

I did this to protect my girls and their reputation. It kept them from being embarrassed at school if they said no. Personally, I didn't care if these boys thought I was a jerk. In fact, I kind of liked it. (*Don't mess with her father. He's crazy.*)

Tim asked me to date my daughter. He seemed to be a young man of integrity, and because of this, I found him trustworthy to date my daughter. (As a side note, for you men who have high school daughters: It is your job to make sure your daughter's boyfriends are trustworthy.)

When Tim first asked if he could date my daughter, he had already been to our house several times. I had a good read on him, and he loved God. When he asked to date my daughter, I told him that, like all dating relationships, there was a chance this would not work out. How he would handle that, if it happened, mattered greatly to me.

"You will handle any breakup with respect, integrity, and honor," I told him. "You will not call her to breakup, text her to breakup, or any other form of communication except in person."

Now, at the time, Tim was a United States Marine. In every physical sense, he was superior to me. I acknowledged this in our conversation. I said, "You are taller, stronger, and faster than I am, but if you do not handle the relationship with my daughter properly, I will hunt you down, and those attributes won't matter because you can't outrun a .45 caliber bullet."

I got the response I want: "Yes, Sir!"

Integrity leads to trustworthiness. In this case, I eventually gained a son-in-law for whom I have the utmost respect. He is a man of integrity and an absolutely trustworthy husband to my daughter.

And he never had to outrun a bullet. (Smart man!)

**Someone Else's Money**

Two of the stewards in Matthew 25 were trustworthy, and one was not. How did that happen?

Have you ever thought about the history of these three stewards and the money that was entrusted to them? They must have worked for the master for years. They were the top financial performers in his organization. They knew how to invest, manage risk, and take profits at appropriate times. They were chosen because they demonstrated trustworthiness and outperformed their peers. But when the master trusted them with his wealth, their true natures were revealed. Two servants were trustworthy and doubled their master's money. The third was not trustworthy but lazy regarding his master's money.

As the steward of A Plus Powder Coaters, I see this at times. We have had employees who really shine when I am walking through the buildings. They hustle and look busy. But when I'm gone, they take long breaks and look for reasons not to work. If I watch the cameras in their areas, I see they are goofing off. They are not trustworthy. I cannot trust them to do a job efficiently when I am not present. This lack of trustworthiness points to a lack of integrity.

If we are going to steward God's wealth, we must be trustworthy. When God speaks about doing something with his finances, we need to respond and demonstrate that we are trustworthy. When I am in a church service, and they are receiving a special offering, Laurie and I pray and talk about how much we should give. When we come up with a number, I have to be trustworthy to give that amount in the timeframe that meets the need. I can't have second thoughts later and retract my commitment. If I tell the pastor we will meet a need, they need to know they can trust me to send the money.

In the last chapter, I told you about Terry and his successful sales career with A+. He has also been a trustworthy employee. I have told many people, "Terry treats A+ like it is his."

Now, that statement could be read two ways. One way implies that he brags to everyone that he is the owner. That is not the case. The way I mean it is this: Terry has always treated A+ as though it reflects his personal integrity. He handles every situation as if A+ bears his name.

When Terry was in charge of production, and there was a breakdown, he would get a price on a replacement part and ask me if he could buy it. Yet I didn't need that level of micromanagement. "It's just a twenty or fifty-dollar part," I'd say. "Buy it and get a spare as well. That inexpensive part could cost us a whole day's production."

But Terry didn't want to be presumptuous and spend A+ money without checking with me. Because of this tendency, I developed a lot of trust in Terry. He proved himself trustworthy.

Over the years, as A+ has grown, God has placed many people with integrity and trustworthiness in our management team. I am so blessed that I can travel and speak at conferences, knowing that the men and women on my management team will handle the daily situations that could come up. I trust them not to embezzle, defraud, or do anything else that would jeopardize A+.

My top three people who report directly to me are amazing.

- Terry Watson is our Sales Manager.
- Nick Sukosd is our Operations Manager.
- Heather Reilly is our Office Manager.

Each one exhibits the qualities of integrity and trustworthiness. A+ would not be what it is today without such an amazing management team. Yet truth be told, they are also my friends and part of my A+ Family.

At the next level of management, we have:

- Melanie Sprouse is our customer specialist.
- Steve Trimacco is our quality manager.
- Tyler Ogden is our estimator.

This group also has impeccable integrity and trustworthiness.

I could go on and on about the integrity-based trust I have in the A+ family. Integrity and trust are vital in business relationships, but they are even more important when stewarding what God has entrusted to us.

**Prayer**

Lord, help me to be trustworthy with all that you have entrusted to me. Help me remember that what I am stewarding is yours, and that I need to be able to be trusted with it if I am going to steward more someday. Please help trustworthiness to grow in me and be part of who I am. Amen!

# 11

# Generosity

IT IS INTERESTING how we expect the church to be generous, but not ourselves. When people are in need, we suggest they talk to the church. Why? Because we think the church is supposed to take care of people. Certainly, that is true, but our understanding of the church is wrong. We are the church! Not the building we meet in on Sunday. Not the staff of the church we attend. Church is the one you see when you look in the mirror. Jesus was talking to people when he said:

> *Give, and it will be given to you. Good measure, pressed down, shaken together, running over, will be put into your lap. For with the measure you use it will be measured back to you.*
>
> Luke 6:38

It is good to be a giver.

There are two things I would like to point out about this verse.

1. If we give, it will be given back to us according to "the measure we use." In other words, if we give a lot, we will get a lot. If we give a little, we get a little. The more we give, the more we receive. There is no minimum or maximum. We could give a penny or a million dollars. Either way, we will receive it back proportionately: "pressed down and shaken together." We see an increase in what we gave.

2. One might assume this scripture is talking about giving to the church in the form of a tithe, offerings, alms, or first fruits. Now, I

believe it applies to these areas, but it also applies to everything else. This scripture tells us we should be generous givers in everything we do.

Following Luke 6:27-31, we see this message in context.

> *But to you who are listening I say: Love your enemies, do good to those who hate you, bless those who curse you, pray for those who mistreat you. If someone slaps you on one cheek, turn to them the other also. If someone takes your coat, do not withhold your shirt from them. Give to everyone who asks you, and if anyone takes what belongs to you, do not demand it back. Do to others as you would have them do to you.*

This reads like a lesson in overall generosity, not prescribed giving. "Give to anyone that asks," appears to include forgiveness, mercy, and forfeiture of personal property rights, including one's cheek.

The lesson continues in Luke 6:32-35

> *If you love those who love you, what credit is that to you? Even sinners love those who love them. And if you do good to those who are good to you, what credit is that to you? Even sinners do that. And if you lend to those from whom you expect repayment, what credit is that to you? Even sinners lend to sinners, expecting to be repaid in full. But love your enemies, do good to them, and lend to them without expecting to get anything back. Then your reward will be great, and you will be children of the Most High, because he is kind to the ungrateful and wicked.*

We are to love our enemies. That can be hard at times, especially to give to our enemies. Yet Jesus explains why these lessons are so important. From Luke 6:36-37:

*Be merciful, just as your Father is merciful. Do not judge, and you will not be judged, Do not condemn, and you will not be condemned. Forgive and you will be forgiven.*

In verse 38, we finally arrive at where we started. With the context well established, we see the full meaning of Jesus' statement on giving—not just what happens when we give, but how to give and what to give. Turns out, everything is on the table.

*Give and it will be given to you. A good measure, pressed down, shaken together and running over, will be poured into your lap. For the measure you use, it will be measured to you.*

This scripture is talking about the characteristics of a Christian—how we should act. Yes, our actions get a response from God, but what are those actions? Take a look at this table.

| **Our Action** | | **God's Response** |
|---|---|---|
| Be merciful | → | God will be merciful |
| Don't Condemn | → | You won't be condemned |
| Don't Judge | → | You won't be judged |
| Forgive | → | You will be forgiven |
| Give | → | It will be given to you |

Notice that Jesus said nothing specifically about giving money to the established church. Instead, he broadened our understanding of what giving really looks like. We need to be givers of our lives, and if we want a greater return, we need to be generous givers.

**Everyday Generosity**

Tipping the Scales

We need to be generous in everything we do. When we go out to dinner, are we generous tippers? Do we tip the expected amount, which is about 18%? Are they blessed by you? Or are you just another customer?

When I give a standard 18%, I am just a customer. Someone they won't remember. They are unimpressed. It's another day, another dollar, and we quickly fade from memory.

Now, had we tipped 50%, we would have gained their attention. They would remember us and be eager to see us again. Generosity like that is impactful.

So, why is that important?

Tipping is the tangible currency of approval. This gives us an audience with them. It opens the door for us to tell them about our lives, including Jesus and our faith.

Generous giving gets their attention long term. They know you tip well, so they are willing to engage with you. It impresses them enough that they want to know more about you and why you are so generous.

Laurie and I are creatures of habit. We go to the same few restaurants most of the time. We are on a first-name basis with most of the waiters and waitresses. They are eager to see us. Over time, we move from just being a customer to being on a first-name basis. Laurie and I now look for opportunities to share Jesus with them.

One young lady was pregnant, and we got to share in the excitement of her pregnancy. We told her we would be praying for the baby. Another server was going through a loss. We prayed with them in the restaurant.

Our giving opens doors to introduce Jesus into their lives.

I've read that food servers hate working Sunday lunch and Wednesday night dinner because that's when the Christian crowd comes in, they (we?) are the worst tippers. Some even leave a tract—a small booklet explaining the Gospel—in place of a tip.

As Christians, we think we are leaving them life-changing information, and we are. Just not the message we intended. The problem is, the garbage cannot be read, and that is where that tract ends up. It turns them off from Christ more than it intrigues them.

An article on tipping showed a restaurant receipt on which a Pastor wrote: "I only give God 10%. Why would I give you 18%?"

Reading that, I was embarrassed to be a Christian. Not embarrassed by Christ, but embarrassed to be affiliated with such a poor mindset. That pastor is not representing Jesus well. Aren't we supposed to be Jesus' ambassadors? Displaying him to the world? What God are we representing? My God is generous to me. He doesn't just meet my needs; he exceeds them.

I want non-believers to see that God is generous, so I am generous with them.

## Gifting Strangers

While having dinner, we will often buy a gift card and write something about Jesus, saying God loves them and wants to bless them. Nothing too lengthy. When we leave, we will either give the card to the hostess or our waitstaff and ask them to give it to a random customer.

I was recently on a plane and noticed a woman hand the stewardess a gift card. She told her, "Thank you for taking care of me." That inspired me. I should carry gift cards and bless the stewardesses on my flights. Maybe with a little note about Jesus or an encouraging word.

How else can we be generous?

Give to the homeless. Honestly, I often struggled with giving to the homeless for several reasons.

One: Why don't they just get a job? And please don't say there aren't any. As a business owner, I know of lots of companies hiring at any given time. I wanted to hand them an application instead of money.

Two: They might spend my money on alcohol or drugs. I don't want to fuel their destructive lifestyle.

But as I have pondered my reason for not giving, it dawned on me: Jesus didn't say give to the poor with strings attached. We don't control what they spend the money on. Rather, we are told to give, and it will be given back to us. Scripture says to give to the poor, period.

> *Give, and it will be given to you. A good measure, pressed down, shaken together and running over, will be poured into your lap. For with the measure you use, it will be measured to you.*
>
> Luke 6:38

My daughter and I were recently talking about giving. God was convicting her to give to the poor, yet she struggled. Her stance on the subject was that the poor should get a job, and she didn't want to give to someone who might use the money to buy drugs or alcohol. (Gee, I wonder where she got those ideas?)

I shared what the Lord brought to my attention through Luke 6:38, that it isn't my responsibility to control how someone spends my gift. My job is to give generously. A true gift is for the receiver of the gift to decide how to spend it. That is between themselves and God.

My daughter felt led to give to the poor, holding signs at a Walmart near her. Yet she didn't know how to do it and stay safe. We came up with the idea of putting the money or gift card in an envelope with a card that shared her faith. She could slide it out of the window without putting the window all the way down. Just low enough for the envelope to slip out. She feels safer yet is also able to bless the poor.

It is funny how my daughter and I had that talk just days after the Lord convicted me to be generous to the poor. I now make sure I have cash with me to give to the poor when I am out and about. I want to bless those begging at intersections.

**Negotiating Generosity**

As a business owner, I get a lot of requests for donations. I find there are many ways I can be generous. We try to give wherever we can. But what about when we deal with our suppliers? Do we beat them up on price for every penny we can get?

I did that for many years until I realized it is God's money, not mine, and he wants me to be generous. Does price matter? Yes. But I try not to beat the vendor up by pressing for cheaper and cheaper pricing.

As a competitive negotiator, I found myself looking for a win by getting the price as cheap as possible for the company. I had no regard for how it affected the vendor as long as I got the win.

I now go for win-win. I evaluate their price and ask:

- Is that fair for both of us?
- Am I driving them out of business?

- Will the vendor be eager to do more business with me?
- Have I built a relationship or strained one?
- Will they see Jesus in me when the deal is done?
- Did I represent Jesus as a generous God?

**Employee Generosity**

As with most business owners, I count the cost of giving our employees raises. As of this writing, we have about 80 employees, so to give a dollar-an-hour raise to each one equates to $80/hour, or over $100,000 a year. When I look at that number, it can be scary. Indeed, it's a big number. Yet I have to ask: Am I being generous with what I am offering them? Is their wage generous for comparable companies in our area?

Back in about 2001, I wanted to give our employees a raise. Yet we were not profitable, so we had no extra to give. As I prayed about what to do, I felt God ask a couple of things:

- Am I willing to show favor to my employees?
- Did I have enough faith to trust him in giving a raise when I didn't have the resources?

I brought all the employees into the showroom. We had ten employees at the time. I told them I really couldn't afford to give them a raise, but I felt God told me to give them a raise anyway, so their next check would reflect an increase. I didn't realize it at the time, but God was testing my faithfulness and generosity. Within a short time, we went from losing money to making money.

Generosity paid off! Give, and it will be given to you. (I think I read that somewhere.)

**The Master's Happiness**

Generosity is a character trait we develop. It's something we work on. Having the right stewardship mindset is important to developing generosity. The idea that all I have is God's, not mine, frees us to be generous. We need to remember: God isn't running out of money. He is a good and generous provider to us. We need to be generous towards others.

Now let's tie this back to Matthew 25:20.

> *The man who had received five bags of gold brought the other five. "Master," he said, "you entrusted me with five bags of gold. See, I have gained five more." His master replied, "Well done, good and faithful servant! You have been faithful with a few things; I will put you in charge of many things. Come and share your master's happiness!"*

Now, this phrase, "Come share in your master's happiness," implies generosity from the master—a reward for doing well. Clearly, the master is a good master, just as our God is a good God! We know he will give a generous bonus if we do the same.

Speaking as a businessperson, if you had doubled my five bags of gold for me, I am sure we would celebrate. I wouldn't hand you a fifty-dollar gift card to Longhorn's and say, "Well done," or even "Medium rare." No. I would take you and your wife on a first-class trip to Hawaii or Aruba. We would celebrate. You can't really celebrate and not be a little generous.

### A Fair Price

A couple of years back, I was looking for a 1976-79 Chevy Blazer or GMC Jimmy. I found one in Southern California. I messaged the person and got their number. It was a woman who had driven a 1978 GMC Jimmy for several years, but it needed some work, and she didn't have the money. She was asking $9,500 for it. That was a fair price, assuming the truck wasn't rusted out. All I really wanted was the body and frame.

We talked for a few minutes, and I asked if she could send me additional pictures. She didn't know how. So we FaceTimed so I could see the vehicle.

The Jimmy looked pretty clean. I could see chips in the paint, yet there was good metal behind the chips. I made what I thought was a fair offer, considering I could not see the vehicle in person, and it might end up only being worth a few thousand dollars. She said no, that she had a higher offer. I asked what it would take to buy it. She said $8,500. I said, "Give me a few minutes, I'll call you back."

We hung up, I prayed, and I felt God say buy it.

The Jimmy arrived in Ohio a few weeks later. Wow! The metal body was in great shape. She called and asked me to send her license plate back, as she forgot to take it off. As I took it off and looked at the Jimmy, I knew it was worth what she had originally asked for it. So I wrote a check for $1,000 (making up for the reduced price I had negotiated) and sent it to her with a note saying the Jimmy was worth her asking price of $9,500. I wanted to be honorable and generous to her.

She called me in tears. She told me that she spent the money from the Jimmy on a reliable car, but her septic tank now needed repairs, and the cost was fifteen hundred dollars. She had five hundred dollars but had no idea where to get the other thousand until my check showed up. I got to share with her about God and how he had told me to send her the money.

As I look back on that situation, I remember what I tell my children when they get upset about something. "In ten years, will this still upset you?" This applies to our generosity and finances. In ten years, will the extra thousand I spent on the Jimmy matter? Will it impact my life? No. But it impacted that woman's life for years to come.

## Generosity In Practicality

This same principle about paying extra for something happened at A+ about fifteen years ago. We owned four acres, and there was a vacant strip of 3.3 acres next to our property. A developer owned it. I didn't need the land at the time, but knew if we continued to expand, we would run out of room without it. I reached out to the owner, and he said he would sell it. He wanted $100,000 for the land—that was just over $30,000 an acre.

My problem was that the acreage around us was going for $20,000 to $25,000 per acre. I didn't want to pay any more than that. I tried to make offers, but he wouldn't budge. Finally, I paid his asking price of $100,000.

First, I realized that in ten years, the higher price wouldn't matter, especially if the business expanded onto the land, as I expected.

Second, expanding the business would cost me a lot more than the extra I paid for the land if I had to move the business.

My point: Don't be afraid to spend generously on things.

Now, I am not saying to overspend when you don't have it, but I am saying when you have the resources, don't worry if you spend extra. Being generous is a good thing, even a prudent thing, and God honors it, especially when he sees a future we don't see.

## Be Like God

Our generosity is a direct reflection of how we see God's generosity. If we tend to be stingy, we view God as stingy. If we tend to be generous, we view God as generous. If you feel there isn't enough to be generous, or that God hasn't been generous with you, I encourage you to ask God to show his generosity. Ask him to change your perspective to make you generous.

**Receiving**

When I was younger and starting to make a better wage, I wanted to be generous. So, when we went out to dinner, I would buy for those who were with us. I really enjoyed blessing others. In fact, if someone else tried to take the bill, I would insist on buying.

One day, Joy, one of our pastors, mentioned that a true giver also needs to be able to receive. *Wait, what?* So, I started praying about it and realized I needed to learn to receive. I have had to learn to let others buy my dinner and simply thank them for their generosity.

This does a couple of things.

One: It helps me stay thankful for their blessing and keeps me from having to be the "Big Man" who buys everyone's dinner.

Two: It allows others to be blessed through giving. "Give, and it will be given…."

I needed to learn to share the reward for giving and not hog it all for myself. A generous giver also needs to be a gracious receiver.

**Prayer**

Lord, forgive me for being stingy with your resources. I realize that everything is yours and that you are a generous God. Help me to be generous and represent you, any chance I can. Help me to be able to receive from others and be thankful for their generosity. Amen!

# Part IV

# Applications

# 12

# Joseph—A Good Steward

JOSEPH FROM THE BIBLE was a good steward. We know of Joseph from the book of Genesis. Joseph was his father's favorite son. And as it typically goes, Joseph was also the youngest (at the time) and was born to his father, Israel, in his old age. In Genesis 37, Israel gave Joseph a colorful robe.

Now, his brothers already hated Joseph, and this didn't help. *Dad just gave him a special coat.* Then Joseph had a dream (verses 5-7) about stalks of wheat. One stalk rose to the top, and the others bowed down to him. Joseph said he was the top stalk, and his brothers were the lower stalks bowing down to him. Now they really wanted to kill the little squirt.

In verse 9, Joseph had another dream. The sun, the moon, and eleven stars bowed down to him. He said this was his brothers and parents bowing down to him.

Clearly, Joseph knew a lot about dream interpretation, but personal survival was not high in his skill set. His brothers were now burning with rage.

One day, his brothers were out grazing the sheep, and Israel sent Joseph to check on them. When they saw him, they decided to murder him and tell Dad that his favorite son had been killed by a wild animal. (More like 11 wild animals.) But at the last minute, they decided to sell him to a caravan that was passing through and heading to Egypt. Joseph was sold to Potiphar, one of Pharaoh's officials and the captain of the guard.

> *Now Joseph had been taken down to Egypt. Potiphar, an Egyptian who was one of Pharaoh's officials, the captain of the guard, bought him from the Ishmaelites who had taken him there.*
>
> *The Lord was with Joseph so that he prospered, and he lived in the house of his Egyptian master. When his master saw that the Lord was with him and that the Lord gave him success in everything he did, Joseph found favor in his eyes and became his attendant. Potiphar put him in charge of his household, and he <u>entrusted</u> to his care everything he owned.*
>
> Genesis 39:1-4

Potiphar entrusted Joseph with everything he had. We said earlier that stewardship is the careful management of something entrusted to one's care. Joseph was set in a position of stewardship.

> *From the time he put him in charge of his household and of all that he owned, the Lord blessed the household of the Egyptian because of Joseph. The blessing of the Lord was on everything Potiphar had, both in the house and in the field. So Potiphar left everything he had in Joseph's care; with Joseph in charge, he did not concern himself with anything except the food he ate.*
>
> Genesis 39:5-6

Potiphar left everything he had in Joseph's care, and "with Joseph in charge, he did not concern himself with anything."

This means Joseph was *trustworthy*. There is no other way to describe Joseph than that he was trustworthy to handle everything Potiphar owned.

When someone is truly trustworthy, you have no concern for what they oversee. You completely trust in what they are capable of handling. You don't second-guess them. You don't check up on them. You know they have your best interests in mind. Unfortunately, Joseph's honor was about to become a liability in the corrupt Egyptian society.

> *Now Joseph was well-built and handsome, and after a while his master's wife took notice of Joseph and said, "Come to bed with me!"*
>
> *But he refused. "With me in charge," he told her, "my master does not concern himself with anything in the house; everything he owns he has entrusted to my care. No one is greater in this house than I am. My master has withheld nothing from me except you, because you are his wife. How then could I do such a wicked thing and sin against God?" And though she spoke to Joseph day after day, he refused to go to bed with her or even be with her.*
>
> Genesis 39:6-10

Joseph's stance represented integrity. No one would know if he slept with his boss's wife. It would have been their little secret. But Joseph had *integrity,* and he knew God would know. He would lose his favor with God and his Egyptian boss, and he didn't want that to happen.

Still, temptation persisted. Verse 10 says, "And though she spoke to Joseph day after day, he refused to go to bed with her or even be with her."

Joseph didn't even want to be around her. I'm not talking about sleeping with her, which he didn't want to do, but he didn't even want to be in the same room with her. Why? He knew that there was a temptation, and he avoided it.

Do we avoid temptation? Avoidance is part of integrity. It is not putting ourselves in a situation where, at a weak moment, we might give in and lose our integrity. Joseph put safeguards in place to protect his integrity. He avoided as many compromising situations as he could.

Do we put safeguards in our lives that protect our integrity? For me, as a businessman, I don't hold meetings where I am alone with a woman. I would never want things to appear that anything inappropriate was going on. I also don't want to put myself in a situation where something inappropriate could happen. When female salespeople need to meet with me, I either have Heather, my office manager, or Nick, my operations manager, sit in the meeting.

Unfortunately for Joseph, there is an old saying: *Hell hath no fury like a woman scorned.* Potiphar's wife tried to get up close and personal with him. She grabbed Joseph's robe. Joseph had a choice to make: give in and lose his integrity or RUN! He left his robe in her grasp and escaped butt-naked. How embarrassing. Well, I suppose he had his underwear on. But still….

Potiphar's wife then lied to Potiphar and said Joseph tried to rape her. Whether he believed her or not, Potiphar threw Joseph in jail. Not much of a reward for having integrity.

> *Joseph's master took him and put him in prison, the place where the king's prisoners were confined.*
>
> *But while Joseph was in prison, the Lord was with him; he showed him kindness and granted him favor in the eyes of the prison warden. So the warden put Joseph in charge of all those held in the prison, and he was made responsible for all that was done there. The warden paid no attention to anything under Joseph's care, because the Lord was with Joseph and gave him success in whatever he did.*
>
> Genesis 39:20-23

While in prison, Joseph was put in charge of all the prisoners. From verse 23: "the warden paid no attention to anything under Joseph's care." Here again, Joseph was operating with *integrity* and *trustworthiness*, so that the warden didn't even have to pay attention to him. The warden had no doubt Joseph would do what was right.

The fruit of integrity is that others trust that you will do what is right. They never wonder what you will do; they are confident you will do the right thing.

Things were about to turn around for Joseph. He was doing his thing in prison when Pharaoh had a dream that no one could interpret. The Pharaoh's cupbearer remembered Joseph, who had interpreted his dream. Joseph stood before Pharaoh and told him God's meaning of the dream. This impressed Pharaoh to no end.

> *Then Pharaoh said to Joseph, "Since God has made all this known to you, there is no one so discerning and wise as you. You shall be in charge of my palace, and all my people are to submit to your orders. Only with respect to the throne will I be greater than you."*
>
> Genesis 41:39-40

**Joseph in Charge of Egypt**

Because Joseph had integrity and was found trustworthy, he was elevated beyond Potiphar's household. Joseph was put in charge of all of Egypt under the Pharaoh, and everyone submitted to him.

> *So Pharaoh said to Joseph, "I hereby put you in charge of the whole land of Egypt." Then Pharaoh took his signet ring from his finger and put it on Joseph's finger. He dressed him in robes of fine linen and put a gold chain around his neck. He had him ride in a chariot as his second-in-command, and people shouted before him, "Make way!" Thus, he put him in charge of the whole land of Egypt.*

> *Then Pharaoh said to Joseph, "I am Pharaoh, but without your word no one will lift hand or foot in all Egypt."*
>
> Genesis 41:41-44

Joseph moved up the stewardship ladder to second-in-command of Egypt. Had Joseph given in to temptation and lost his integrity or not been trustworthy with the things entrusted to him, he would not have advanced.

Yes, it was unfair that Potiphar's wife lied against Joseph. How many of us would have accepted the punishment and its setback? We'd have grown bitter and said, "Look what integrity and trustworthiness got me! Imprisoned! I give up on those qualities. From now on, I'm looking out for old number one! Me!"

But that is not the attitude of someone with true integrity.

We must realize that the enemy is against us. When we have integrity and trustworthiness, there will be seasons when we are tested. How we handle it—how we come through it—will determine whether we can be trusted with more. Joseph advanced in stewardship because he never wavered in his integrity or trustworthiness.

We need to make integrity and trustworthiness part of our stewardship foundation.

Fast-forward to the end of the story. True to Pharaoh's dream, a famine hit the region, but Joseph heard from God and had stored up lots of grain. Meanwhile, back at the ranch, food was scarce for Israel and his family. So Israel sent his sons to Egypt to buy grain—the very brothers who had sold Joseph into slavery. They came before Joseph and didn't recognize him, but he recognized them. They wanted to buy grain, and Joseph accommodated them, yet with a catch.

> *Joseph gave orders to fill their bags with grain, to put each man's silver back in his sack, and to give them provisions*

> *for their journey. After this was done for them, they loaded their grain on their donkeys and left.*
>
> Genesis 42:25-26

Joseph was *generous*. He didn't sell the grain; he gave it to them. Eventually, Joseph revealed himself to his brothers and reconciled with his family.

> *But Joseph said to them, "Don't be afraid. Am I in the place of God? You intended to harm me, but God intended it for good to accomplish what is now being done, the saving of many lives. So then, don't be afraid. I will provide for you and your children." And he reassured them and spoke kindly to them.*
>
> Genesis 50:19-21

How easy it would have been to be bitter at his brothers for selling him into slavery and separating him from his dad, who adored him. But instead, this steward had integrity, trustworthiness and generosity. And his final act of character was expressed through forgiveness. He was the bigger man.

We need to be the bigger man or woman at times. Take the high road. Maintain our integrity. Stay trustworthy. Be generous, even when we do not want to.

# 13

# Poor or Wealth Mindset

People who struggle financially typically have a poor mindset. They have been poor for so long that they think and act like poor people. We are all like that, to a certain extent. We should be aware of this mindset and contrast it with a wealth mindset. The two mindsets are very different.

- Poor Mindset: Just need enough for today; never thinking of tomorrow/future.
- Wealth Mindset: Always planning with the future in mind.

Which one are you? More accurately: to what extent are you one or the other? When you think of finances, is it in terms of today's needs or future needs? Is your goal to have just enough for today and not worry about tomorrow until it gets here? Wealth-minded people are always thinking about how the money they have will impact their future.

Poor Mindset:

- Spends the cash as soon as they get it.
- Lives paycheck to paycheck.
- Money burns a hole in the pocket.
- Buys most things on credit.
- The debt cycle never ends.
- Ends up in further dependency

Wealth Mindset:

- Has a plan for money (budget).
- Pays bills on time.
- Saves and invests, no matter how little.
- Saves for the items to purchase.
- Pays cash.
- Operates with little or no debt.
- Realizes sacrifice now pays off in the future.

See the difference in the two mindsets?

When I worked full-time at the Therm-O-Cel Company, we got our checks every Friday at noon during our lunch break. I remember an employee with two young kids and a wife. They lived at a poverty level. At one point, they lived in his car in the parking lot. Every Friday, he cashed his check, loaded up the family, drove to Dairy Queen, and bought everyone a big meal, including fries, milkshakes, and sundaes.

By Monday, he was broke. He had no food for lunch and had to borrow five dollars for gas. I often thought, if he would stop taking the family to Dairy Queen, go to the grocery store instead, and buy a couple of loaves of bread, some peanut butter and jelly or ham and cheese, he could have fed them all week on what he spent at Dairy Queen. Yet his poor mindset had him trapped in "spend it now before it is gone."

******

- Poor Mindset: People spend impulsively.
- Wealth Mindset: People spend strategically.

Poor-minded people must have things now, even if they have to borrow to get them, regardless of the family going without basic necessities.

Wealth-minded people don't impulse buy. They may want something, and if they decide they need it, they save until they have enough for it. They won't borrow for it if they can possibly avoid it. They know it is worth waiting for.

An older sister of mine graduated from college and moved away for several years. She decided to get an accounting degree to better her earning potential. She moved back in with my parents and attended a local college. To support herself, she found a job with a private lender. She wrote loans for people who just needed a few thousand dollars.

She told me that December was the busiest month. A lot of people from the local General Motors plant sought $3,000 to $5,000 loans for Christmas gifts.

Now, these people made $70,000 to $100,000 at their jobs, but they borrowed to buy Christmas presents for their families. They were not smart borrowers. The only question they asked was, "What is my payment?" They never asked about the interest rate, which was 28%. They just wanted to know the payment and duration. They would receive their $3,000 with plans to pay for this Christmas over the next three years.

The following December, they would return to borrow again for the current Christmas. They hadn't paid off the previous loan; they still owed two years, but "I need presents this year." So, they rolled the loans together into a new three-year loan for this Christmas. This repeated year after year. It was a cycle that typically ends in bankruptcy.

******

- Poor Mindset: Lives beyond their means.
- Wealth Mindset: Lives below their means.

People with a Poor Mindset are always trying to live above their means. They want more than they can afford. If a store will sell them something and finance it over a twelve-month period, they will borrow to have it today. Prosperous people, on the other hand, live below their means. If they have extra, they don't have to spend it. They will save it, invest it, or (*drum roll...*) give it!

******

- Poor Mindset: Ignorant of the power of finances.
- Wealth Mindset: Understands the power of finances.

Money has power. The government knows it. That is why they love giving free stuff to people. They can influence their votes on Election Day. Money brings power. Look at the news. Do they interview poor people or millionaires? It doesn't matter if the millionaire is an idiot or the smartest person in the world; they get to say their opinion as if it is the absolute truth, and people believe them because of the influence of money.

******

- Poor Mindset: Increase in wages, increase in spending.
- Wealth Mindset: Increase in wages, increase in savings, investments.

Have you ever wondered why NFL players have financial struggles in retirement, even with an $840,000/year minimum wage? The average career of a football player is 3.3 years. You'd think that would be enough time to amass a lifetime's supply of wealth.

It's the same with NBA players. Despite a $1,272,870 minimum wage and an average career of 5 years, many players struggle after hanging up the hoops.

Why are some of the highest wage earners in our economy crashing on the rocks of financial insecurity? Simple, really. As their wages go up, so does their spending. They understand football and basketball, but the more money they make, the more it dribbles through their fingers. They end up in bankruptcy, crying foul as the judge ejects them from the court because of their poor mindset.

Lottery winners have the same problem—an increase in cash brings an increase in spending. Unfortunately, spending is easy. Stewardship requires skill. (*Maybe somebody should write a book about it.*)

Here's how I learned about this firsthand.

The year Laurie and I were married, I was making $14,000/year. Like all good couples, we scraped and struggled to make ends meet for the first couple of years. Then I got a 50% pay increase. We spent it all. A year later, my wages doubled. Sure enough, our spending increased accordingly and we still had no savings. Instead, we had a new van, we went out to dinner a lot, and we bought a boat. *Yee hah!* A poverty mindset can be a lot of fun...for a while. The old saying: *You can't buy happiness, but you sure can rent it.*

A few years later, my wages doubled again. Coincidentally, so did our spending.

Now you might think we would have started saving, but we didn't. Then one day it dawned on me: *I make great money and we have no savings or investments. I work hard to make money. I need to make money work hard for me.*

From that day forward, Laurie and I made a conscious decision to start saving and investing. We went back to a budget. We started saving for the items we wanted. We chose to live below our present means, buying only what we needed and a few of our wants. And we were determined to invest.

I was also fortunate enough to know someone who was knowledgeable about investing, and he guided me in buying stocks.

We planned for our future, knowing that if we sacrificed now, our lives would be much better in the long run.

Because of our investments, when we had the idea to start A Plus Powder Coaters, Inc., we had the money to start our new business. Had I kept my "spend everything" mentality—which was a poverty mindset in disguise—I never would have had the resources to start A Plus.

Thank God! We learned not to be impulsive in our purchases and instead learned to grow our money and live below our means. Less is truly more!

******

- Poor Mindset: I can't afford that.
- Wealth Mindset: How can I afford that?

Years ago, I read *Rich Dad, Poor Dad,* by Robert Kiyosaki. It is not a Christian-based book, but it teaches good principles. The premise of the book is that Robert's dad was poor, and he taught Robert how to live as a poor man. Yet his friend's dad was rich, and he taught Richard how to make wealth. So, Richard learned from two dads: one poor and one rich.

His poor dad would say, "We can't afford that." End of subject.

His rich dad would say, "How can we afford that? We can't afford everything right now, but we can figure out a plan so that eventually we can afford it. We can increase our earning power. We can save and plan until we can afford it."

Quite a difference in approach.

The fact is, a poor mindset leads to poverty, and a wealth mindset leads to prosperity.

Here's an example of how a poor/poverty mindset and a wealth/prosperous mindset view things differently.

**By the Numbers**

Let's say someone gives you $1MM to do whatever you want. Like most people, you begin buying things for you and yours.

You decide to buy a bigger house. Now, you don't want to be too greedy, so you settle on an above-average house for $600,000. (As of this writing.)

Well, your car is falling apart, so you spend $60,000 on a nice SUV.

You have always wanted to go to Israel, so you and your spouse decide to splurge and go first class for $20,000.

You want to bless your family (and maybe impress them, if you're honest with yourself), so you buy a few expensive gifts for $20,000.

Being a good Christian, you know you should tithe from the million dollars. That would be $100,000. But you've never written a check that big. You start to have second thoughts. *That's an awful lot of money for the church. Do they really need that much? It might corrupt them. Gee, I'd better pray about this.* Still, you read my other books and realize that if you can't tithe on what you make now, it won't magically change when you have more money. For the sake of argument, let's say you decide to tithe the $100,000.

Totaling this up, you spent $800,000. Yet you still have $200,000 left. You're proud of yourself for not spending it all. (*Wait until Bob hears about that!*)

There is just one problem: Uncle Sam wants his fair share. Because our Federal taxes are on a graduated scale, you eventually end up at the 37% rate, currently, anything over $625,000. That means, in round numbers, you owe $320,000 to the United States government on the $1MM alone for Federal taxes! The $200,000 you had leftover just evaporated, and the IRS wants an additional $120,000.

*But wait! There's more!*

The State wants its income tax on the $1MM. So that's $27,500 (assuming Ohio).

Social Security, you owe $11,439.

You also have Medicare tax of $21,700.

Let's not forget the city tax at 1.5%, so $15,000.

Of course, the school district tax is 1.5% for another $15,000.

You end up owing nearly $400,000 of the $1MM you just received.

Let's not forget the $60,000 you made at your daytime job. That income is now taxed at 37% since you received the $1MM and everything beyond that is at 37% federal.

Good news: You have $200,000 left from your windfall.

Bad news: You need to borrow $200,000 more to pay your taxes. (*On second thought, don't tell Bob, OK?*)

Now, a prosperous-minded person would have done the math OR have hired somebody who knows a whole lot more about finance than you do. Together, they would have realized that they would end up owing $400,000 come April 15$^{th}$. In preparation, they would have set that money aside either in an interest-earning savings account (usually 4% interest) or possibly a short-term investment like a Certificate of Deposit. They want their money working for them. They might also start looking for legitimate tax shelters.

Again, they would seek help from a trusted professional, their bank, and friends with demonstrated track records of stewarding wealth.

If it were I who received this windfall, the second thing I'd do is tithe 10%. The first thing I'd do is thank God for the blessing. The third thing I'd do is determine: *How can I make this money work for me?*

With this understanding, let's look at how prosperous people handle money.

**Attitude Toward Wealth**

When we talk about poor/poverty and wealthy/prosperous, we're talking about property. There is a difference in how poor people and prosperous people see finances. Poor people see it as a way to get what they need now, while prosperous people see it as a tool to grow their finances. Of course, no one is completely in one group or the other. We are all works in progress. Growth means changing how we see money and developing our vision for finances. This, in turn, qualifies for greater stewardship.

Where did the poverty mindset start? Maybe we learned it from our parents. For years, the institutional Church embraced a poverty mindset. The teaching was that it is better to be poor and go to heaven than have wealth and go to hell. This might sound pious to a religious-minded person, but as we discussed at the beginning of this book, it is not biblically sound. In Matthew 27:57, we read of Joseph, who was a rich man and a disciple of Jesus. Deuteronomy 8:18 states that God gives us the ability to produce wealth. There are many more such scriptural references.

So, where did the church come up with the idea that Christians need to live in poverty?

**Lady Poverty**

St. Francis of Assisi lived from 1181 to 1226 and came from a very influential, prosperous family. We are talking billionaire wealth like Donald Trump, Bill Gates, or Elon Musk. He felt his wealth stood between him and God. That wealth had been too important to him, so he gave it all away and took an oath of poverty. In essence, he married

"Lady Poverty." He started the Franciscan Order of the Catholic Church. He was known as "The Little Poor Man."

Now, I am not questioning that St. Francis might have needed to eliminate wealth from his life, but I take issue with the idea that all Christians are to eliminate wealth from their lives.

It might have been what God called Saint Francis to, but it wasn't for everyone. When Saint Francis married Lady Poverty, the poverty spirit entered the church. The church—not just the Catholic Church, but all churches—adopted a poverty mindset. This is a spirit of thinking that says Christians need to be poor. When you have a poor mindset, the root of it comes from the poverty spirit. (Sorry if that stings a little.)

On vacation to the Outer Banks of North Carolina, I read a book about blessings and finances. The author said that God asked him if he trusted him (God) with his finances. When he said yes, God said, "Give me all your savings."

That struck a chord in me. "God, are you asking me the same thing?"

Would I give up my savings to him? Did I love God more than my savings? The short answer is, yes, Laurie and I once gave God all our savings. In doing so, we showed God that we love him more than money. God didn't require us to forgo ever having savings. He just asked us if we would give our savings at that time. So, we did.

Now, that was our story. It would be wrong for me to say, "Everyone needs to give their savings to God." I'm sharing what God called me to do, not everyone.

Another example would be diet. For the last four years, I have been strictly off sugar. I have not had a cookie, ice cream, candy, cake, or pie. The reason is that I struggle with self-control in eating sweets. I can't stop at one cookie. If I have one, I'll eat ten. I finally decided the best thing for me is to just not eat sweets. I eventually became fine with that decision and seldom miss them, but for me to impose that discipline on everyone else would be wrong. (Incidentally, my next book will be titled: *Get Off Sweets and Give All Your Money Away!* jk)

Likewise, the idea that poverty is for everyone is crazy. God may call you to give something up. It might be for a season or even a lifetime, but to put your personal decisions on everyone else is wrong.

The Church has embraced Lady Poverty. They have married her, brought her home, carried her over the threshold, and made a home with her. I think we need to divorce Lady Poverty.

**Go Car Go**

I already wrote about my 2011 Camaro Convertible 2SS/RS. I flat-out loved that car; no other way to put it. But I soon discovered my underlying guilt about it when I found myself making excuses to justify its purchase. My guilt was rooted in a poverty mindset. I secretly believed God was running out of money and resources…and quite possibly Camaros. (*No!!*)

The fact is, God loves giving to his children. He is an abundant giver.

*Take delight in the Lord,*
*and he will give you the desires of your heart.*

Psalm 37:4

*Bring the whole tithe into the storehouse, that there may be food in my house. Test me in this," says the Lord Almighty, "and see if I will not throw open the floodgates of heaven and pour out so much blessing that there will not be room enough to store it.*

Malachi 3:10

Here's another way to look at this. As a parent, your son, Johnnie, starts playing guitar. He has talent. He loves strumming his guitar beneath a tree by the railroad tracks. He dreams of his name in lights. He has a cheap beginner guitar but wants a Fender American Ultra 2 guitar. It costs $2,500, and you don't have it. As a parent, you want to provide the guitar, but you are already financially tight.

Yet you see the desire and yearn to get it for him, so you take an extra shift every weekend. You start mowing a couple of neighbors' lawns for extra cash. You find a coupon for Guitar Center, see that the guitar is on sale, and it's a double-coupon day. You grab the cash you've been stashing, use the double coupon, and buy this beautiful guitar. You give it to Johnnie, and he is ecstatic. Hugs and "I love you" follow. You give yourself a pat on the back. *Finally got something right.*

The next day, you exercise your parental responsibility by eavesdropping as Johnnie's little friend, Chuck, is over. You hear Chuck ask, "Man, where did you get that cool guitar?"

Johnnie responds, "Mom and Dad got a good deal on it. It was double-coupon day and on sale. I know when I am done with it, they will get their money back when they sell it."

Would you feel a little deflated, devalued, unappreciated, and a little hurt? What you intended as a blessing turned into a burden. How do you think God feels when we make excuses for the things he has blessed us with? I think the same as we would feel as a parent, after all, he is our heavenly father.

The fact is, God loves to give us nice things—things that align with our wants and desires as he created us.

In 2017, I built a 1968 Corvette called "Green Mamba." I had a video made about the build and at the end it said something like, "I want to thank God for the time, talent and the finances to build this car. Without God, I am nothing."

The video had over 100,000 views in just a few weeks. One day, I decided to read some comments. One particular comment said, "How many poor people could you have fed with the amount you spent on that car?" Wow, was that hurtful. This person had no idea how much my wife and I give away. They judged that I should not have spent the money on the car but should have fed the poor instead.

First, my wife and I give most of our money away. Had that person asked, I would have told them that. But the real point is, they have a poverty mindset. They think that if I spent the money on something I enjoy, then God doesn't have enough to provide for the poor. That thought is just plain rooted in poverty. The fact is, God does have enough. He has more than enough. What he doesn't have is people who know how to steward the abundance of his giving!

I have a pastor friend who called me and we talked about cars. He was thinking of buying a sports car and wanted some insight into Corvettes. A month or so later, we were talking and I asked if he had found a Corvette. He said no, he was now thinking of buying a Lamborghini. I was excited for him. In fact, I asked if I could have a ride if he got it. (I really hope he lets me drive it.)

My point is: Do you have a problem with a pastor having an exotic car? If so, why? Because people in ministry are supposed to be poor? Sacrificing finances for ministry? They shouldn't have expensive things because God doesn't have enough for that? That is a poverty mindset.

We need to celebrate when our friends, pastors or people in ministry do well or have nice things. We can't let jealousy, envy, or a poverty mindset or poverty spirit take control. It is time to change our poverty mindset to a prosperous mindset and celebrate when God blesses us or others with wants (which are things above and beyond what we need).

Here is a simple prayer asking God to forgive us for doing something he hasn't called us to do.

**Prayer**

Father God, forgive me for embracing Lady Poverty in my life; for thinking you have called me to poverty when you have given me the ability to produce wealth, as it says in Deuteronomy 8:18. I trade my poverty mindset for a prosperous mindset. I receive the ability to produce wealth. In Jesus' name. Amen.

# 14

# Vision and Timeline

I LIKE PRACTICAL STEPS—things I can do to implement what I have just learned. I typically conclude my speaking engagements with ideas people can do to practice what they have heard. This book is no different. I want to give you a few tools to become the best steward you can be. It starts with vision.

> *Where there is no vision, the people perish.*
>
> Proverbs 29:18 KJV

We need to start with a vision for our future. Robert Herjavec has a great saying. "A vision without a timeline is just a dream."

Is stewarding of more wealth just a dream, or is it a vision? Sitting on the couch and hoping for money to fall into your lap is dreaming. We need a vision, a plan, a strategy if we are going to steward more wealth.

People with a prosperous mindset and good stewardship skills plan for their future. They are prepared for whatever the future may hold. This was the essence of Jesus' parable of the ten virgins in Matthew 25.

> *At that time, the kingdom of heaven will be like ten virgins who took their lamps and went out to meet the bridegroom. Five of them were foolish and five were wise. The foolish ones took their lamps but did not take any oil with them. The wise ones, however, took oil in jars along with their*

> *lamps. The bridegroom was a long time in coming, and they all became drowsy and fell asleep. At midnight, the cry rang out: "Here's the bridegroom! Come out to meet him!"*
>
> *Then all the virgins woke up and trimmed their lamps. The foolish ones said to the wise, "Give us some of your oil; our lamps are going out."*
>
> *"No," they replied, "there may not be enough for both us and you. Instead, go to those who sell oil and buy some for yourselves."*
>
> *But while they were on their way to buy the oil, the bridegroom arrived. The virgins who were ready went in with him to the wedding banquet. And the door was shut. Later the others also came. "Lord, Lord," they said, "open the door for us!'*
>
> *But he replied, "Truly I tell you, I don't know you."*
>
> *Therefore keep watch, because you do not know the day or the hour.*
>
> Matthew 25:1-13

Notice that five of the virgins had a plan. They prepared, thought things through, and even anticipated setbacks. The other five lived without a plan. They flew by the seat of their pants (OK, by the hem of their robes), hoping it would all work out and they would get to the bridegroom and his party.

Which one are you? The planner who anticipates? Or the dreamer who merely hopes things work out? If you want to prosper, you need a plan. You may not be the best planner, but there are resources that can help you: books, professional planners, and even the Holy Spirit. You need to plan instead of just hoping things work out.

What's a plan look like? I'm glad you asked.

### 1, 3, 5, 10 Year Plan

Start with a layered approach ranging from short-term to long-term. Make a 1-, 3-, 5-, and 10-year plan. Now, I know 10 years sounds like a long time from now but think back ten years ago. It seems like yesterday, doesn't it? (Hair today, gone tomorrow.)

#### Year 1

This first year is about getting your spending under control. This means developing a budget and beginning to pay down credit card debt and high-interest debt, like payday lenders. It pains me to even say "budget" because too many people become legalistic over precise control of every cent. A budget is a tool to help us discipline our spending habits. It allows us to examine our present spending and gauge our long-term trajectory. (We will go into more detail on our spending later.)

#### Year 3

All credit card debt is paid off, and we have a savings account started. We no longer buy on impulse but think judiciously about whether we can afford the items we are considering. We also start making extra payments on our house. If you have a thirty-year loan on your home and make one extra payment a year, it will shorten the payoff by six years.

#### Year 5

Our spending is all intentional. We only buy with cash. We have been making extra payments on the house. Our cars are paid off. We have a savings account for a new car, so we can pay cash when the time comes to trade in our clunker. We have enough savings to start investing. We set up college funds for our kids. We can start thinking about retirement.

**Year 10**

Our house is paid off. Our only bills are utilities and food (and the mortgage burning party we threw with our friends and family). Our investments are growing. We have discretionary funds, so we can buy a few things we have always wanted: new bicycles for the kids, dinner out once a month, and a yearly vacation to Florida. Life is good!

**Your Mileage May Vary**

These are ideas. Your plan may vary. Indeed, it should vary. Ask God for his wisdom in developing a doable plan for you and your family. Ask your pastor if there is anyone at church who is good with finances that might help you. Seek a reputable financial planner.

Bottomline: Do something. Do a lot of things. If you do nothing, in ten years you will be in the same place…or worse. And your kids will never get those new bicycles.

# 15

# The Decision

WHAT IS STOPPING YOU from stewarding at the next level? What is your ceiling of faith for the wealth you could be stewarding? Here's a hint: It's that person staring back at you every morning, right above the sink.

We are the ones who limit what we can steward financially, not God.

**Reactive vs. Proactive**

Here's a recent revelation that changed my life. I realized that for years, I was stewarding my resources from a *reactive* perspective instead of a *proactive* perspective. In other words, I was focused on stewarding at my present income level—reacting to the challenges at hand.

The problem is that I'm being told prophetically that God is preparing me for greater wealth. My challenge, then, is learning to steward at my future level. For example, disciplines that might seem trivial at the level of average wealth suddenly become vital—even a matter of survival—as God entrusts us with greater wealth. People think that more wealth brings ease and comfort. To a degree, it does. But left to our own devices, it can destroy us. Only when we steward wealth God's way can it be a blessing to us and to his kingdom. And that, my friends, is an acquired skill.

But recently, I have had some prophetic words that financial increase is coming for Laurie and me. Big increase. I have been praying into that, asking God to prepare me for that level, that it would not go to my head, that I would not become consumed by what God entrusts to me. I don't want money to become mammon—the idol of wealth.

> *No one can serve two masters; for either he will hate the one and love the other, or else he will be loyal to the one and despise the other. You cannot serve God and mammon.*
>
> Matthew 6:24 NKJV

While praying into our future level of stewardship, I have also been asking God for insight and wisdom on how to grow what I currently have.

I mentioned earlier that people tell me they want to be like me someday. Yet they don't know me. They only know what they see. They are really saying: "Someday I hope to have your wealth."

One of my nephews said as much at a family gathering. "Uncle Bob, I want to be like you someday." I was flattered, but what he and other people see is that Laurie and I live a good life. We have a beautiful home, a successful business, travel first class, and I have several classic cars. But what they all fail to ask is how I got here. It wasn't like one day, I magically became wealthy.

No, it was through hard work, applying God's principles to my life, and being teachable.

People rarely ask how I did it and what I've learned. They just want the result. Which is a start, I guess. But admiration only gets you so far. If left unchecked, it becomes envy, jealousy, and finally despair.

This is especially true in America. We want everything now. Hot food in a minute from our microwave oven. Fast food from the drive-thru because we are on the go. *Who has time to cook?* We are impatient. Demanding. Entitled. *Forget the process. Just give me the results.*

**Get It Done**

How many times have we run into someone we haven't seen in a long time and notice that they are looking fit and trim? We compliment them, and inwardly, we decide *I'm going to get in shape like them.* Then it hits us: *We have to diet and exercise.* So, we make a New Year's resolution to lose weight. Never mind that it's only April. *Hey, baby steps, right?* Maybe we join a gym. Subscribe to the Fitness Channel. Make big plans to walk daily. *I'll start tomorrow.* Then tomorrow comes, and we say, *I'll start tomorrow*. It starts to sound like a tear-jerker on the Hallmark Channel: *Tomorrow Never Comes.*

Our resolve wanes. We go three weeks of half-hearted attempts and don't look any better, so we console ourselves with a burger, fries and a milkshake. Best we've felt all month! Still, we're right in line with the average person. Only 10% of people follow through with New Year's Resolutions.

As you might suspect, Jesus had a different take on goal setting. From Matthew 13:

> *Later that same day, Jesus left the house and sat beside the lake. A large crowd soon gathered around him, so he got into a boat. Then he sat there and taught as the people stood on the shore. He told many stories in the form of parables, such as this one:*
>
> *"Listen! A farmer went out to plant some seeds. As he scattered them across his field, some seeds fell on a footpath, and the birds came and ate them. Other seeds fell on shallow soil with underlying rock. The seeds sprouted quickly because the soil was shallow. But the plants soon wilted under the hot sun, and since they didn't have deep*

> *roots, they died. Other seeds fell among thorns that grew up and choked out the tender plants. Still other seeds fell on fertile soil, and they produced a crop that was thirty, sixty, and even a hundred times as much as had been planted!"*
>
> Matthew 13:1-8 NLT

Many people think this parable is about salvation, and it is. But it's also about completing a task…like a New Year's resolution. Let's break it down.

******

> *Some seeds fell on a footpath, and the birds came and ate them.*
>
> Matthew 13:4 NLT

These are the people who never start. They may like the idea, even think they need to do it, but never start the journey. For the unsaved, they hear the Gospel and do nothing about it. *I need to get saved one day.*

From our fitness example, they desire to lose weight and get in shape, and they may say on Monday, *I'm going to start my diet*. Yet Monday comes around, and *Oh look! It's fifty-cent wing night. I'll start tomorrow.* But they never start, and after a few days, they give up because they are just winging it.

******

> *Other seeds fell on shallow soil with underlying rock.*
>
> Matthew 13:5 NLT

In salvation, they decide they need Christ in their lives. They may start reading the Bible and praying for a few minutes a day. After a few days or weeks, however, they feel no different, so they stop.

From our fitness example, they are people who are psyched up, ready to tear it up at the gym, and go on a zero-carb diet. After a few days or weeks, however, they are on to their next self-help program or have completely lost interest in getting into shape.

******

> *Other seeds fell among thorns that grew up and choked out the tender plants.*
>
> Matthew 13:7 NLT

These are the new Christians who last a few months, maybe even a year. But that special feeling isn't there any longer. They face trials in their lives, and they abandon their faith.

From the fitness example, they start eating healthily and hitting the gym a few times a week. They see some results and continue for a while. Then they get invited for a burger and fries with their friends. Their friends are out of shape and eat what they want. *Look at them! At least they're happy!* They choke out the desire to fulfil any fitness goal. They quit going to the gym and start going to burger night with their friends every week.

******

> *Still other seeds fell on fertile soil, and they produced a crop that was thirty, sixty, and even a hundred times as much as had been planted!*
>
> Matthew 13:8 NLT

These are the Christians who have a life-changing experience. They move from a religious mindset to a relational mindset. They want to know Father God, Jesus and the Holy Spirit. They can't get enough of God.

From our fitness example, they change their mindset on how they want to look. They have a long-term vision for their life. They see the big picture. They don't diet; they change their eating for good. They are realistic in their expectations and goals. They know they can't lose one hundred pounds in six weeks; that requires a one-year goal.

They continue exercising. They have a plan, a goal, and they commit themselves to it.

**Patience for Progress**

You have to decide what kind of soil you will be.

- The "nice idea but never start" kind.
- The "lasts a few weeks/months" kind.
- The "form a vision for the future, develop a realistic plan, and execute it" kind.

When we teach our children to drive, we don't put them in a Corvette ZR1X with a zero-to-sixty speed of 1.68 seconds. No, we put them in our oldest car that is easy to drive, and we won't lose our lunch if they put a ding in it. Someday, they may be able to drive a Corvette if they steward their driving and finances. There are multiple levels of advancement to be a safe driver with that much horsepower. The odds are quite high that someone without good driving skills would get killed in the Corvette. It has more power than they know how to handle. You must work up to that level of power, maybe even take some classes on driving performance cars.

The same is true with managing wealth. We have to work our way up, read books on finances, learn to steward at each level, not start at the top, or it may ruin our lives.

Growing in stewardship means starting with what you have. After a while, you find yourself on the next level, stewarding a little more. You prove yourself faithful with that level, and you go to the next level. Picture it like an eternal set of stairs. You are continually going up a level. The only ceiling is the one of your own makings.

# 16

# Practical Steps

HAVING ESTABLISHED A TIMELINE of the changes we need, here are some things we can do both in the natural and spiritual to effect change in our finances

The first thing we need to do is repent for not stewarding God's provision well. Repentance is a matter of asking God to forgive us and then committing to change. In this case, we need to turn away from a poverty mindset—one that says God is not able to meet all our needs. There needs to be a shift from expecting God to provide to asking God to provide. As I stated earlier, we need to ask God to meet our needs. If our furnace is broken, we need to pray, "Father God, your house has a broken furnace. What will you do about it?" In this way, we will allow God to meet our needs.

Now that we have repented and made things right with God, we need to be intentional about change. This starts with asking God to teach us how to steward, both at our current level *and* at the level to which he is taking us.

**Buy Intentionally**

If you want something, wait a week or more. Do you still want it? Need it? Or is it something you could live without? If you buy it, will you still have money for your obligations? Your grocery bill? Your electric bill? Your savings and giving?

If not, then don't buy it.

### Don't Hoard

A budget is a good tool. Dave Ramsey offers excellent online budgeting classes. A budget helps us identify (and rectify) our bad spending habits. But stewarding is more than a budget. We need a balance between a budget and what God is telling us to do with our resources.

If we are hoarding our money, we are not being good stewards. Recall the servant who buried his master's money in the ground. He protected it, but he didn't hear: "Well done, good and faithful servant." That went to the good stewards who operated in faith, accepted risk, and doubled their master's money.

It's dangerous to hoard money. Yes, money is seed, but it doesn't grow in dirt. It grows in investment. (That's why we have money laundering.)

### Live Accordingly

An important thing to change is to live within your means. In other words, live with what you can afford. It doesn't mean you can never dream of something special. Rather, it means you might have to wait for it. That is tough in America. Commercials are geared towards instant gratification. "You can have it now! Just $500 down, $500 a month, for 500 years!"

The seller knows most people will never pay off the loan. So, they continue getting their 28% interest or more on the money they loaned. All so "you can have it now!"

### Plan Ahead

You need a new washer. The old one just danced across the floor, spewing soapy water. *Oh no! New ones start at $500.* Yet you probably knew that old was on its last leg. This was not the first time it did the Macarena. So, did you start saving and planning on replacing it? That is where a good budget comes into play. It enables you to set aside money for emergencies and regular maintenance.

**Marital Bliss**

It is important that you and your spouse are on the same page with your newfound stewardship goals. I have been very blessed to have a wife who doesn't like to shop or spend money. I am the impulsive buyer in the relationship. We had to learn to be on the same page with our finances. Not surprisingly, finances are the number one thing couples fight about. Get on the same page with your finances. Seek help if need be, counseling, marital, and financial. The sooner, the better.

Related to this is my strong recommendation to a) marry wisely, and b) cultivate your marriage. Nothing will drain your bank account and keep you in poverty like a divorce, especially if child support and/or alimony are involved. Often, the legal split is the final act in a series of bad decisions. Yes, fighting over money can eventually land you in divorce court, but the wealth (and the marriage) is usually gone by then.

**Save Baby Save**

Start a savings account by setting an amount of money aside for emergencies, big purchases, or future wants. This goes back to planning your spending. Be proactive instead of reactive.

As you start saving money, you will find that you have some you can invest. You will need to investigate what investments you are comfortable with. A lot will depend on how much risk you are willing to take. My dad told me, "Never invest what you cannot afford to lose."

There is truth in that statement. As with most investments, there is a chance you could lose some or all of your investment. Fortunately, relatively safe investments exist, and they will pay off.

As you are reading these words, there is somebody, somewhere, reading about using OTM: "Other People's Money" to advance their goals. That is what investing does. It provides capital to others, and they pay you for it.

Read and learn all you can before investing. And do not eschew the services of reputable investment professionals. Start small, perhaps with mutual funds. Diversify. Don't bet it all on the next Apple startup or a literal pot of gold. Embrace a tolerance for risk, but choose your risk wisely. Good investment is a marathon, not a sprint. Finally, do not succumb to greed. Greedy people make bad decisions, and bad decisions make you broke.

**Downsize**

Maybe you need to sell some nonessential wants you purchased. Things you wanted but didn't really need. Did you know one-third of people who buy exercise equipment never use it? But they had to have it. Free up some cash and sell it.

Maybe you financed a fancy zero-turn mower and are making payments on it. Sell it and buy a used mower. The exercise will do you good.

And if you ever fell for the high-pressure sales of buying a timeshare, get rid of it! (There are companies that can help you.)

**Increase Your Income**

Start making yourself more valuable to the marketplace. Look for a job that has potential for advancement. You might have to take a wage cut to get in the door, but it's worth it for long-term advancement.

I am amazed at how short-sighted most of us are when it comes to job advancement. *If they paid me more, I'd work harder.* No, you wouldn't. Well, you might for a week or two. But it wouldn't last. The truth is that hard work precedes advancement. Not every company will see your value, but you don't have to stay there either. You are free to look for gainful employment elsewhere.

The point is: Excel where you are, even as you seek other opportunities. You never know who your next boss will be. It could be the business owner you are waiting on at McDonald's. You have no idea who is looking for good employees on the other side of the counter. How you deal with them could change your whole future.

But if your attitude sucks because you hate the job, it will show when you serve people. You could eliminate the potential for a better opportunity, all because you thought the job you had was beneath you. Are you better than that job? Prove it. Excel your way up and out. Anybody can quit. Few can rise.

**Increase Marketability**

Maybe you need to increase your knowledge or credentials. Finish that college degree. Enroll in a trade school in the evening. Earn a Project Management Certification. Take night classes or online classes. Learn to weld. Acquire a second language.

By doing so, you increase your worth to a company and, more importantly, to the marketplace. Some companies will pay for your schooling. Even if they won't, grow in your knowledge and expertise.

Here's how it works: Your wage is not determined by your employer. It is determined by the marketplace—what someone else is willing to pay for your skills and experience. Your present employer pays the least amount necessary to acquire and retain someone of your capabilities. This is normal business.

The better you do at your present job, the more valuable you will appear to a prospective employer.

**In the Nick of Time**

Let me share a couple of job opportunities from our company.

Nick was a manager of a small restaurant that Laurie and I frequented. As a business owner, I watch people, see how they interact with others, and how they solve problems. My mind rarely rests.

Nick stopped at every table. He made sure everyone was taken care of. One particular night, they were very busy with people lined up at the door. The busboy was cleaning a table and clearly overwhelmed. I watched to see how Nick would handle this. Would he yell at the busboy to *speed it up? People are waiting*! Or would he take charge and enact a solution?

To my amazement, Nick grabbed a container, cleared a table, wiped it down, and then had the hostess seat the next customers in line. He solved the problem by getting involved.

I was impressed. I am always looking for problem solvers. The next time I was at that restaurant, I gave Nick my card and said, "If you want to change careers, call me."

He called the next day. I interviewed and hired him.

Do you know what the most impressive thing about Nick's hiring is? When I asked when he could start, he said he needed a month to finish the holiday season and train a replacement for his job. That is dedication, and that is something I wanted for A+. I hired Nick as our quality manager and estimator. He is now my operations manager. He answers to me, and most of the other managers answer to him. He had no idea that I, as a customer, would be his next boss. He was stewarding well what God had given him, and it paid off.

**Play Well**

I play guitar on our worship team when I am in town. The church was having a conference that started on October 31st, and our regular bass player couldn't make it. Our worship leader asked Stephen, from another church, if he would play during the conference. I met to practice with him before the conference, which started on Friday night. After practice, I introduced myself to Stephen. Nice guy, and a good bass player. I didn't think much more about him.

After the conference, we were putting our instruments away, and Stephen and I started talking. He said he needed to find a new job. I asked why. He told me that they had a company Halloween party that night, and they brought in someone with Tarot Cards for entertainment.

"I can't work for a company that does that," he told me.

I asked what he did. He was in Safety and HR. My ears perked up. Nick, our operations manager, had been telling me we needed a Safety and HR person so we could be more intentional in these people-sensitive areas. So, I invited him for an interview with Nick and me. We hired him.

He had no idea that playing bass that night would lead to a new job for him.

**Work Hard**

I have given some examples of working hard and getting noticed by others. But what about in the company you are currently in? I am big on promoting from within when possible.

Steve was a young man, just out of high school. We hired him as a basic laborer. He worked hard. He would volunteer for overtime, cover for other people, do whatever was needed. We needed a second shift foreman. The management team had all noticed Steve, so he was the pick. He did an excellent job. Later, our quality manager put in his two-week notice. Who did we move to that position? Steve was the overall pick. He had done well as a foreman and showed the attention to quality that we needed in a quality manager. Hard work paid off for Steve.

I was taught to work hard. My attitude was that you do whatever is necessary to get the job done.

As I said earlier, I started my career at fourteen, working for the local Ace Hardware store, fixing broken windows and screens and stocking shelves. I strove to be my best at the job.

Returning to my story of my first factory job, when I turned sixteen, I got a job in a local manufacturing facility called Therm-O-Cel Company. I was just summer help, but I worked as hard as I could. They taught me to drive a forklift, and I quickly became their best forklift driver. The foreman did all the repairs on the equipment, so I offered to help, and he taught me to weld and repair the equipment. When they needed someone to stay over, I volunteered. I gave one hundred and ten percent every day I was there.

When Laurie and I got married in 1984, I was still just a laborer in this small company. The week I was to be married, my foreman came and told me he had gotten me a dollar-an-hour raise. I told him to get lost. I was busy and didn't have time for his clowning around. He stopped me and said he told the owner that I was much more valuable than the $4.85/hour I was making, and that another company would surely see my value. If he wanted to keep me, he should give me a raise.

Hard work had paid off. I got promoted to assistant foreman in this small shop. I still did a labor job, but if the foreman was on vacation, I filled in for him. I did most of the repairs and just kept working hard.

A few years later, the owner (who was my dad) wanted to retire. He offered me the opportunity to purchase a third of the company. Not only did he offer me this chance to own a third of the company, but he also financed it. My hard work had paid off. I went from grunt to business owner in about ten years' time.

Work hard, and it will pay off.

**Sowing Principle**

I believe in the sowing principle. I do not want to belabor this point. The Bible tells us to tithe, give alms, give offerings, and first-fruit offerings. Therefore, we need a plan for giving. If you say, "Well, someday I'll tithe, but I just can't afford it," you never will be able to afford it. You will never tithe or give. But it is key to seeing an increase in our finances.

> *"Bring the whole tithe into the storehouse, that there may be food in my house. Test me in this," says the Lord Almighty, "and see if I will not throw open the floodgates of heaven and pour out so much blessing that there will not be room enough to store it. I will prevent pests from devouring your crops, and the vines in your fields will not drop their fruit before it is ripe," says the Lord Almighty. "Then all the nations will call you blessed, for yours will be a delightful land," says the Lord Almighty.*
>
> Malachi 3:10-12

> *Give, and it will be given to you. A good measure, pressed down, shaken together and running over, will be poured into your lap. For the measure you use, it will be measured to you.*
>
> Luke 6:38

The key to increase is to give of ourselves, our energy, our faith, and our resources. When we give, we receive an increase. When we are generous, we receive a generous increase. These are just a few practical steps you can take to be on your destiny to seeing an increase in your finances.

(For more on this, see my book: *Created to Make Wealth.)*

# 17

# Growing Wealth

HOW DOES WEALTH GROW? There is a simple formula that I was taught in school, The Rule of 72. It says that if you divide 72 by any interest rate, it will tell you how many years it takes to double your money.

Example: if you invest your money at 4%, the math says: 72/4=18. It will take eighteen years to double your money.

The past couple of years, the average return on stocks has been just over 10%. So if you divide 72 by 10, your money doubles every 7.2 years.

**Do the Math**

Let's say you were eighteen when you got your first job, and since you live in your mom's basement and pay no rent, you decide to spend that time playing video games. *What? No!* You read my book, come to your senses, and decide to save $10,000 and invest it at 10%.

In just over seven years, that $10,000 is now worth $20,000. In another seven years, it will be worth $40,000. In another seven years (just over twenty-one years), it will be $80,000. Let it grow for a total of 50 years, and you can retire a millionaire with $1,280,000. All from a one-time investment of $10,000 when you graduated from high school.

Parents, tell your child that when they first start working, they can live at home for free if they put $10,000/year in investments. They will retire a millionaire, and you can kick them out or charge them rent. Of course, by then, they'll be choosing your nursing home.

Here's another idea. If you invest $1,000 a year at 10% earnings for 30 years, you will have $168,000 at the end of those 30 years. All from a $30,000 investment. Now, maybe you are thinking you can't afford $1,000 a year. If you break that down to monthly, it is $83.33/month for 30 years. That seems like an easier number. But what if you broke $1,000 down to a weekly investment? It would be $19.23/week. So, at the end of 30 years, earning 10% interest, your weekly $19.23 becomes just over $168,000.

We sometimes think we need a large sum of money to invest. But we can start with twenty dollars a week.

Now, I am not a financial investment expert. I have no hot stock tips for you. I encourage you to find someone who is good with investments and learn from them. Maybe you need to read about investing or take a class. Just be careful, and ask yourself: *Does what they say make sense? Can I verify what they are advising me to do?*

# 18

# Final Thoughts on Stewardship

I HAVE APPLIED stewardship primarily to finances, but these principles apply to all areas of our lives.

**Marriage**

God has been challenging me to steward my marriage better. So I have been working on developing a deeper connection with Laurie. I have been stepping out in faith, taking a risk, and telling her my innermost thoughts. I want an increase in our relationship and am working towards that. I am trustworthy and have integrity in our marriage. I am trying to be more generous with my time with Laurie. I even ask God, "Lord, this woman of yours, how can I serve her better? How can I encourage her and see her fulfill her destiny?"

Some of you might be praying about your marriage a little differently: "Lord, the spouse you gave me is broken. What are you going to do about it?"

Truth be told, it is sometimes the person praying who is the broken one. I don't pray for God to change my wife. I pray that I can fulfill my husbandly responsibilities to love her, cherish her, and encourage her to fulfill her destiny.

**Spiritual Life**

Another area of my life that I am intentionally stewarding is my spiritual life. I am working on reading and better understanding the Word of God. I am stepping out in faith and sharing what I feel God is saying or doing in situations. I maintain my integrity and trustworthiness by not wavering in my faith or compromising who God has called me to be.

**Parenting**

How well do we steward the children God has entrusted to us? This has been an area of intense involvement for me, as it is for most parents.

- Am I parenting the way the Lord wants me to steward?
- Am I seeing growth in my children?
- Do I work at helping my children grow?
- Am I encouraging my children to be generous?
- Am I teaching my children what true stewardship is?

There are times we might pray, "Father, these children of yours are wearing me out. What are you going to do about it?"

Children are a great joy to steward, although there will be times when you will question it. This is where integrity and trustworthiness step in, and you press through.

**Attitude of Gratitude**

The other day, Laurie thanked me for "letting her" buy some new shirts.

I said, "Honey, you don't need to thank me. Buy what you want."

She said, "I feel spoiled by what I can buy."

That's when it hit me. The difference between spoiled and not spoiled is gratitude. Spoiled people feel entitled, deserving, and demanding what they feel is owed to them. They are never satisfied with what they have. Unspoiled people have an attitude of gratitude.

Two people could have the exact same things; one is spoiled and one is not. Gratitude keeps us from being spoiled. It keeps us in a place of appreciation for what we have.

I start each day walking and praying. One of the things I do is to thank God for our tangible blessings: a beautiful home, the furnishings, the heat and air conditioning, hot water (I love long, hot showers), the nice cars, the garages, my shop, the classic cars and race cars, and the beautiful piece of property where we dwell with deer, eagles, and other wildlife. I don't take these things for granted. I want to stay in a place of appreciation for them.

Let me conclude with a scripture that I think about a lot.

> *For when you have become full and wealthy and have built fine homes to live in, and when your flocks and herds have become very large, and your silver and gold have multiplied along with everything else, be careful! Do not become proud at that time and forget the LORD your God, who rescued you from slavery in the land of Egypt.*
>
> Deuteronomy 8:12-14 NLT

"Do not become proud…and forget the Lord your God." This is why I am so grateful and show so much gratitude to God. I don't want to forget what he has done for me. I see this scripture this way:

> *For when Bob has become full of rib-eye steak and is wealthy and has built his dream home on the lake, and when A Plus Powder Coaters has become very large, and his stocks, bonds, silver and gold and car collection have multiplied along with everything else, be careful! Do not become proud at that time and forget the LORD your God, who saved you from death, destruction and Hell.*
>
> Deuteronomy 8:12-14 BBV (Bob Bertelsen Version)

I obviously preach a lot on growing wealth. I believe it is scriptural. But I also believe wealth can distract us from God. It can become our security. We can let wealth replace God when we have everything we think we need. That's when we start thinking we don't need him.

Truth be told, the more wealth I steward, the more I press into God to make sure God is still first and will always be first in my life.

**My Prayer for You**

I pray this book has brought new revelation to stewarding. I pray you grow in the ability to steward. May you be found: "Well done, good and faithful servant," and be put in charge of more!

May your ceiling be removed, and you start climbing the levels God has set before you. Amen!

Onward and upward!

# About the Author

Bob Bertelsen has over 30 years in business and founded his current company, A Plus Powder Coaters, Inc., in 1996.

He has worked diligently to develop a great culture in his company where the employees have established the values of respect, attitude and quality. A Plus Powder Coaters, Inc., was named Business of the Year in 2016 by the Columbiana, Ohio Chamber of Commerce, and named Manufacturing Business of 2025. Bob credits this award to his employees for their values and culture. Bob mentors several businessmen, helping them establish Godly principles in their companies. He has spent many years on the Custom Coaters Steering Committee for PCI (Powder Coaters Institute) and served as a director of the Columbiana Chamber of Commerce for many years.

One of Bob's passions is being a good steward, something that has been on his heart for over 25 years. He has spoken at various churches and seminars on stewardship, giving and finances. Bob considers himself a "Financer of the Kingdom," a person created to make wealth to partner with ministries to fund their needs.

In his spare time, Bob races and builds vintage race cars. He is currently racing his 1968 Corvette and has won many national autocross events.

Bob and his wife, Laurie, currently reside in Columbiana, Ohio. They have three adult daughters. Bob and Laurie are a part of Real Living Ministries in Boardman, Ohio.

Bob can be reached at his website:

finishlineresources.com

# Resources

Thank you for reading my book. Here are some of the things you will find on the website: finishlineresources.com

- Home "Decree of Ownership"
- Business "Decree of Ownership"
- Ministry "Decree of Ownership"
- Audio files
- Videos
- Pictures of the fire in 1988
- Info on Bob Bertelsen
- More about Bob's Racing
- Updates on new books and resources
- Contact info for speaking engagements

God gave us the ability to produce wealth. God showed me over twenty years ago that I was to be a financier of the Kingdom—someone who brings the finances to a ministry for the ministry to not only survive but flourish. No ministry can exist without money. I knew my calling was to make wealth and honor God with it. I also realized I am not the only one created to make wealth. I believe there are thousands, if not tens of thousands, of men and women of God who are called to make wealth. This book is about that calling.

I am a third-generation business owner. My grandfather started a company in the mid 1940's and passed away shortly after, leaving my dad to take over in his twenties.

I have grown a lot as a businessperson, and my perspective has changed over the years as to what works and what doesn't work in business. In my present company, A Plus Powder Coaters, Inc., I have watched it emerge as a forerunner of what a Christian company should look like.

Being a businessperson is a calling from God. As such, we need to honor God with our business and how we run it. I hope and pray this book causes you to view your company in a new way. May you embrace your calling as a businessperson and honor God with your company.

# Help Us Reach Others

Thank you for reading my book, *Ain't Your Money.* If you have enjoyed this book and feel it has been helpful, would you take the time to go to Amazon.com and write a review? The review will help others see the value in this book and fulfill their callings as Christian Entrepreneurs.

Amazon.com

(Use your cell phone camera to scan the QR code to take you to the website)

www.ingramcontent.com/pod-product-compliance
Lightning Source LLC
Chambersburg PA
CBHW071340230926
51846CB00002B/404
*9781968924010*